To Alison.

You may never be able to read this, but you are the reason that this book has even come into being.

Thank you for teaching me more than I could ever hope to teach you.

Notes from the Author

WE ARE ALL people in process. God meets us where we are and moves us along this slow and often painful road to becoming the image of His Son.

We are also parents in process. No one taught us how to be a parent. We learn, develop, and change our methods over time. For those of us with special needs children, no matter what the disability our child has, we are in the process of learning how to parent a child with a disability. Each of us knew we were having a baby, but chances are good we didn't know we were going to have a child with special needs. So after we get over the shock, the grief, the anger, and the denial, we pick ourselves up and begin the process of becoming a parent to this child.

Now you've decided to home school. So now you are also a teacher in process. Although I have been a professional teacher for over twenty-five years, I am still learning, growing, and changing my ideas and my beliefs about teaching. Each child I teach is a new learning experience for me. I have also labored for over fifteen years to create a home school that met the educational needs of my children while still getting the kitchen and bathrooms cleaned on a semi-regular basis and maintaining a relationship with my husband! So I know where you are coming from!

This manual is intended as a framework to aid you in teaching your special child at home, but it will not give you all the answers. Teaching is hard work, but teaching special needs children has uniquely discouraging aspects to it. Growth can be painfully slow, pressure from yourself and/or outside people can be intense, and most of our children are resistant or have other difficult behaviors. You have taken on a task that is definitely not for the fainthearted, and it is very easy to get discouraged.

I'd like to share a verse with you that has been very helpful to me in keeping my perspective as I teach, "Whatever you do, do your work heartily, as for the Lord rather than for men; knowing that from the Lord you will receive the reward of the inheritance. It is the Lord Christ whom you serve" (Col. 3:23 NASB).

Special Note for the Third Edition

This book originally came out when I was expecting my youngest child who is now fourteen years old! Throughout this book, you will see mentions of my children at various ages. As this edition goes to print in 2008, Alison is now twenty-one, Laura is twenty and Logan is fourteen. Many things have changed over the years, but the basic principles that I have used in over fifteen years of home schooling and have used with countless families remain the same. Therefore, although resources have been updated and new sections have been added, the bulk of the book remains unchanged from the original.

I have now experienced almost every stage of home schooling from preschool to high school, from multiple children to only one at home doing school. And we have experienced the many stages of having a child with severe disabilities from diagnosis to conservatorship. I hope that whatever stage you are at – just beginning or seasoned veteran – you will be blessed and encouraged as you read.

Contents

SECTION TWO: TACKLING THE ISSUES

SECTION THREE: PLANNING YOUR PROGRAM

SECTION FOUR: CHOOSING CURRICULUM

Acknowledgments

For the third edition

EACH YEAR, THE number of families contacting us for help in home schooling their special needs children grows. I could never hope to meet the needs of these families alone. God has provided a wonderful group of women who have come alongside this ministry to keep it running and keep the families we work with supported, encouraged, and organized! Thank you Becky, Elaine, Kathy, Lea, Pam and Roneta – I absolutely couldn't do this without you all.

A special acknowledgement also must go to my mother, Janene Crawford, for this edition. When it was discovered that the digital copy of the second edition of the book had been damaged, she re-typed the entire book so that it could be revised. Wow! Thanks doesn't even begin to cover it. Love you, Mom!

Finally, I want to thank all of the families that I have worked with over the last twenty-plus years who have allowed me to get to know them and their children. I am constantly learning through the process of our collaborations. Thank you for letting me be a part of your home school journey.

Introduction

IN THE COURSE of my consulting work, I received a typical phone call from a mother looking for help. She explained how her daughter had been in public school special education for several years but had made little progress. Convinced by some home schooling friends that her daughter would do "just fine" if they brought her home, she and her husband decided to give home schooling a try. She joined a group of other home schoolers and was told that a certain phonics program was all she needed to "take care of" the poor teaching her daughter had undoubtedly received in the big, bad public school, and that learning disabilities weren't real anyway. So she plunged in and started working, but her daughter still made little progress. At her support group, she tried to voice her concerns but was told that she probably just wasn't working hard enough. So back home she went, feeling just a little guilty, to work even harder.

By the time she called me, she was afraid to ever take a day off school, even for a field trip, for fear of being accused of not working hard enough, and her daughter broke into tears every time the phonics book came into sight. She called to ask me what she was doing wrong, and if I thought her daughter might have a learning disability after all.

When I reviewed this girl's testing, I could see right away that she had a rather severe language processing difficulty. When I tested her myself, I found that she was working almost four grade levels below her "expected" grade, and that phonics was only one of her many difficult areas. She definitely had a learning disability!

In contrast, I was also contacted by another family who was convinced that their daughter had a learning disability. The father was teaching math, and he said that they had tears every day, but she just couldn't seem to understand or remember what they had done the day before.

When I tested this girl, however, I found that there was no learning disability but instead, a very strong preference for visual learning and some difficulty with long-term memory, which meant that she had to see things several times before she could remember them. In discussing the test results with the parents, we discovered that her father's learning style (and, thus, his teaching style) was almost exactly opposite from that of his daughter. Most of their difficulty and frustration had stemmed from the fact that he explained things in a way that was hard for her to understand, and he didn't understand her need for repetition. Once he understood, and we chose some material that fit her learning style more appropriately, everyone was much less frustrated and learning could take place.

These two very different cases illustrate an important fact when we are discussing children with learning problems—there is no one blanket statement that encompasses every child. We need to be careful when we hear statements like, "There are no such things as learning disabilities," or "Children just learn differently. Bring them home, and all their learning problems will disappear like magic!" For those parents out there struggling to teach children who have true learning or more severe disabilities, those sweeping statements cause guilt, pain, and discouragement.

Of course, there are many children, like the girl in my second example, children who are somehow "mis-matched" with the school system, the material being used, the teaching style being used, or who have been slow to mature. And there are those children who have been poorly taught. But, these children are not learning disabled, and usually do show impressive gains when brought home and taught more appropriately. For these families there are great resources already available (see the resource section under Learning Mis-Matches and Weaknesses for specific suggestions).

But then there are those children who have true learning disabilities—perceptual or processing difficulties that truly interfere with the learning process, or more severe disabilities that impact how much can even be learned. Those of you who are currently home schooling a child with a learning problem already know it is hard. Those of you who are thinking of doing it are probably scared and apprehensive. If you are home schooling (or thinking of home schooling) a child with a true disability, this book is written with you in mind.

My goal is to give you three things: basic information, encouragement, and resources. We will start by looking at the facts about the various learning difficulties and disabilities as well as further resources for learning about each type of disability. Then we will address the issues that can prevent us from being effective in our teaching. Finally, we will look at the actual planning of your program, how to identify the areas of need, and choose appropriate curriculum.

Before we begin, I have one word of apology. If you are a father who is the primary teacher for your child, you may feel left out. Because my experience is as a mother, and ninety-nine percent of the families I work with have the mothers as the primary or only teachers, I know that I have used the word "mother" to refer to the teaching parent throughout this book. It seemed cumbersome to keep saying "teaching parent," so I have chosen to say "mother" most of the time. However, I have worked with a number of fathers who were the primary home teachers of their children, and they have all done a fabulous job!

Section One
Getting The Facts

CHAPTER 1

Difference, Difficulty, or Disability?

(What's in a Name)

B EFORE WE BEGIN defining the various learning difficulties, we might as well tackle the "label controversy" head on! I know that many parents of children with learning problems are reluctant to label their children, and phrases such as learning disability, attention-deficit disorder, slow learner, mentally retarded, etc., are viewed with distaste. Since I am going to use these terms throughout the manual, let me explain why I do.

While it is true that a label is not a solution, I am concerned that in our haste to make ourselves more comfortable, we have been left with nothing but a bunch of "politically correct" terminology that is no more helpful than the original "distasteful" labels. Instead of worrying about whether or not a child has a difference or a difficulty or a disability, I believe that what we need, more than anything else, is accurate knowledge if we are to work with our children successfully. Accurate terminology can help when it helps us understand our children's difficulties more fully. What we call something is never more important than what we do, but sometimes our energies can be misspent if we have received an inaccurate impression of our child's abilities and disabilities.

Not only as a professional, but as the mother of a disabled child, I feel strongly that the drive toward "politically correct" language instead of exact terminology more often obscures the true nature of a child's difficulty and actually does more harm than good. For example, I had a family come to me whose child had been given a diagnosis of "developmentally delayed." Taking those terms literally, they went home and proceeded to work as hard as they could to "catch-up" the areas of delay. By the time I saw them, they were exhausted and wondering if home schooling was even working. When I tested this child, I realized that these people were victims of political correctness. You see, "developmental delay" is the PC term for mental retardation. Now if these parents had known that from the beginning, they would have been working in a much different way with this child.

My own daughter was given a diagnosis of severe, pervasive developmental delay. When you hear that, it doesn't sound all that bad, but my daughter is autistic and mentally retarded and that conjures up a whole different set of images, doesn't it! When we "tone down" the terminology of disabilities, we also give misleading impressions of what we, as parents, are dealing with on a day-to-day basis. I'll be honest here; I need people to know as much as possible what I am dealing with because I need prayer and support (and yes, sometimes a little sympathy doesn't hurt!).

One objection I often hear is that if we call all these children disabled, aren't we saying that God made mistakes with them? I think even a quick look through the Bible dispels this idea. Moses apparently had some speech problems, but God says to him in Exodus 4:11, "Who has made man's mouth? Or who makes him dumb or deaf or seeing or blind? Is it not I the Lord?" When Jesus' disciples asked Him who had sinned (a man or his parents) in order that he had been born blind, Jesus answered, "It was neither...but it was in order that the works of God might be displayed in him" (John 9:3).

I have to admit, when I first came to grips with this concept, it made me very angry at God. How could He have made my daughter the way she is on purpose? How could He do that to her, and more importantly, how could He do that to me? However, I have come to realize that as I accept my daughter for who she is, a unique creation of God made for His purpose and pleasure, I have begun to see our circumstances differently. I have come to see (on most days, anyway) that God has given me challenges to face that are molding me into the person He intended for me to be.

By being uncomfortable with the term "disabilities," I think we also give our children a mixed message. We tell them we want them to be unique, but what we mean is that we only want them to be unique in good ways. Our society is obsessed with over-achievement. We don't want even average children, so heaven forbid we should have a child with any disabilities.

When I was teaching English in a regular classroom one year, I had a girl who was very popular and outgoing. She was on the cheerleading squad and had lots of friends. She was a great kid. In my class, she did her work and turned everything in on time, but English was not her strongest area, and she did average work. When grades came out, she got a C. I'll never forget my shock when her mother stormed into my classroom demanding to know why I was out to "ruin" her daughter's chances of ever attending college by giving her a C in my class. When I tried to explain that her daughter had done average work, and that a C was not a failing grade, she screamed at me that anything less than an A was a failing grade as far as she was concerned.

If you think this attitude is rare, it is not. In my years of teaching in private schools, I have seen how our desire for excellence before the Lord has turned into an unrealistic expectation that everyone must be above average. When we encounter a child with a difficulty, we try to minimize that difficulty with obscure language or deny that the difficulty even exists. We desperately try everything we can get our hands on to "fix" our child so that he or she can be "normal."

I admit that I did it too. When my daughter was first diagnosed, I went on the search for the "magic cure." I was obsessed with finding the drug, diet, treatment, therapy, you name it, that would make her normal. Nothing proved to be the cure I sought (although some things did help a little). Finally, one day as I sat on the bathroom floor sobbing, I screamed at God, "Why are there all kinds of books and stories of miracles, but you won't give that to me? Why don't I deserve a miracle? You are so unfair!" But the Holy Spirit brought to mind Romans 9:20 "... who are you O man who answers back to God? The thing molded will not say to the molder, 'Why did you made me like this will it?'" I realized then that I was thinking of my daughter as less because she is different. Accepting the fact that she is autistic and will always be autistic was a big step for me in accepting her as she is—the way God made her. Not a mistake, but Alison.

Now, I can hear many of you saying that this is an extreme example. But while your child may not be as disabled as mine, the underlying issues are the same. No matter what we call the difficulty our child has, we all need accurate knowledge about the difference (difficulty, disability), we all need to accept our children as unique creations of God, and we all need to take appropriate action to teach our children and help them achieve their fullest potential.

Usually I will use the term "special needs child" or "special needs learner" when discussing children with learning problems. The primary reason I use these terms is that they remind me of two truths about our children. First of all, children with learning disabilities of whatever kind DO have special needs. They need more of our time, more of our energy, more of our patience, more of our creativity, and more of our love. But they are also special children—created by God for His purpose and pleasure—just the way they are. It helps me if I don't lose sight of that!

CHAPTER 2

Defining the Various Learning Difficulties

Knowledge, Not Labels

WE NEED TO begin with some brief definitions of the various forms of learning difficulties. There are "official" definitions for each type of learning problem, but as home schoolers, we are not interested in labeling our children for the purpose of qualifying for a program. However, we do need to be informed about the kind of learning interference each child has and how that disability impacts the child and his learning. That's not a label, that's knowledge. And knowledge is power—the power for us to confidently and effectively educate our children with disabilities.

It is not the purpose of this book to explain or discuss every aspect of the various types of learning problems. There are many excellent resources already available for us to learn about our particular child's disability in depth. What I would like to provide is a broad picture of each type of learning problem as a starting point to our becoming more informed about our children.

Some of you, however, are not just starting out. You may have been researching your child's disability for a long time already. If so, these "thumbnail" sketches will be too little information for you, but look over the resources listed. There may be a book that would be helpful to you.

The most important thing to glean from the following summaries or other books is a general picture of how those disabilities typically impact most children. It is, however, important to keep in mind that within each category of disability there are limitless variations—as many as the children themselves. We know our children best. We must not become slaves to the definitions or categories. Often testing for our children will help us pinpoint their exact (and unique) patterns of learning strengths, weaknesses, and areas of interference so that we can plan effective programs (we will discuss testing and planning in depth later).

CHAPTER 3

Learning "Mis-Matches," Weaknesses, and Underachievers

I HAVE INCLUDED this category, even though these are not disabilities, because some of you may think your child has a disability (or you may even have been told that your child has a disability). Instead, your child may simply be mis-matched with the present educational system or material, he may have a specific academic area of weakness without a learning disability being present, or he may be an underachiever. Let's look at each of these possibilities separately.

Mis-Matches

There are several areas in which a mis-match can occur that may look like a learning disability. The most obvious is a mis-match between the learner and the structure. Most often this occurs when the child is in a school situation that is not appropriate to his learning style or needs, but it can also occur at home. Let's face it, not everyone fits the "school mode" of learning each subject for a certain amount of time each day and taking tests at the end of the week. That's not bad, and it's not a disability, it is just a mis-match. These are the children who often "hate school" but love to learn. For example, if you have a very bright child who has a high need for creativity and self-expression who is in a school that uses textbooks for every subject, this student may not be performing up to his potential because the setting doesn't allow for his creative answers or his need to explore the material from a different angle.

This can also happen at home when we structure our home school in a way that is most convenient for us, but doesn't take our children's needs into consideration. Maybe this child needs frequent breaks or to be able to work on one subject as long as he wants. Or, on the other hand, maybe you are a real "unschooler," and your child needs more structure. If you have a child that seems to be bright but bored, try changing the structure and see what happens.

Another potential mis-match is between the learner and the materials. This is an area where we really have to know our children and not allow ourselves to get caught up in every new home school trend that comes down the road. Unit studies may be the talk of the town, but I know children who just plainly prefer workbooks! Also, a particular book or method can get stale after a time, and a change or a break might be in order. Of course, we have to be careful not to go overboard here. Not everything can be fun and games. There are things that we have to teach our children that may not be their favorite but just have to be done, such as learning the multiplication facts or parts of speech.

Mis-matches can also occur between learning styles and teaching styles. The example I gave in the introduction of the very auditory father and the very visual daughter is an example of this kind of mis-match. Even though we may research our children's learning styles, it is good to keep in mind that over time we will just naturally drift toward teaching by our own style of learning. This is why multi-sensory teaching is so often stressed (see the chapter on Choosing Teaching Methods and Techniques for an explanation of multi-sensory teaching).

Finally, mis-matches can occur between reality and expectations. This can be true in several different ways. Perhaps you have a child who is an average learner, but you want a high achiever. Chances are your child is not living up to your expectations and you may wonder if there is a learning problem. As I have already discussed, it is not bad to be average. Sometimes we need to simply step back from the comparison game and accept our children as they are.

Sometimes we can have unrealistic expectations of what home schooling will be like. If you are just bringing a child home, you may be feeling that you are doing this child a big favor by sacrificing your spare time to school him. His view may be completely different! If you are a new home schooler, give yourself and your children time to work into this new lifestyle before you panic and start to think that all your children have learning disabilities.

Finally, remember that children have a very different view of the world than that of adults. The things that you and I deem important are often not viewed that way by our children. Thus, part of education comes down to simple obedience. They must do some things just because we say so. If they complain or dawdle or tell you they can't do it, chances are they aren't disabled, just children!

How do we determine the difference between a mis-match and a true disability? Children who are mis-matched show remarkable gains and differences when removed from the "offending" setting or style. Simple changes with these children produce big pay-offs. This is not true of children with true disabilities. If you bring home a mis-matched child from a school system where he didn't fit, your home school may not run perfectly, but your child will usually seem like a different person. On the other hand, if you bring home a child with a true disability, that disability comes home too. Learning is still hard even if you change the structure or materials or lower your expectations. If that is the case, then testing may help you to determine if there is an underlying interference to your child's learning.

Weaknesses

Other children may be weak in a given area, such as spelling or math, but may not have learning disabilities. This isn't really a mis-match because it doesn't go away with changes in structure or materials, but it may not be a disability either. These learning weaknesses are frustrating to both parents and students, but it is important to keep them in perspective. We all have weak areas. The mother of a child who is home schooled and whose weak area happens to be in academics may feel tremendous anxiety that she is doing something wrong. On the other hand, if this child had a weakness in baseball, no one would panic and rush him in for testing (unless dad has hopes for a major leaguer!). However, many children with mild academic weaknesses are tested for learning disabilities. In fact, if these children are tested in some school systems, they may even be labeled "LD" if the only criterion used is that academic achievement is lower than ability. It is overly broad criteria such as this, with no testing to identify a specific perceptual or processing deficit, that leads to false labeling.

If your child is capable in his overall learning but is weak in a specific area (spelling seems to be the most common one that people call me about), my advice is to not worry about it. I am a terrible speller myself, but I am in no way learning disabled. I have learned to be a better speller over the years (mostly through teaching), but it is not a strength for me. Fortunately, someone created the spell checker, and my life is now easier! The point is that one weak area does not a learning disability make. So don't go looking for more trouble than you have.

Underachievers

Underachievers likewise may look learning disabled if we look only at IQ vs. achievement, but in this case it is only poor motivation or their own lack of personal discipline that keeps them from achieving at their potential. The biggest difference between the child with a specific academic weakness and an underachiever is that typically the underachiever will be doing poorly in all subjects unless something catches his interest while the child with a specific weak area will just do poorly just in that one subject, but be fine otherwise. These are often the children who do well with interest-directed studies or unit studies (see the chapter on Choosing Teaching Methods and Techniques for explanations of these methods). Because of their poor motivation, however, they may tell you that they "don't know" or "don't care" when you ask what they would like to study. However, if you pick something that you know they are interested in and start in on a basic study, you can often catch their interest. I really believe that many of the "miracle" home schooling stories we hear ("My child was making all F's in school. Now we use KONOS and he's four grade levels ahead!") are really about underachievers who have been able to learn when they have interesting materials that seem real to them.

The most effective way to pick out any of these types of children is to test them for perceptual and processing difficulties. I think that testing is always a valuable thing to do if there is any doubt. Many children with legitimate learning disabilities are told that they just need to buckle down and work harder, which is not the case.

What should you do if your child falls into any of these categories? Well, first of all, you can probably stop reading this book! Instead, decide which category your child fits into. If there is a mis-match, see if you can make some simple changes in structure, materials, or expectations. If there is just a specific weakness, look for ways to review or work around that one area. If underachievement is the problem, look for ways to promote motivation. Does your child need a reward system, a change of pace, or have you been lax in discipline and requiring a minimum standard of work? Then check out some of the resources listed below.

False Labeling

What if your child has been labeled LD in the school system, but you think he really belongs in one of these categories? First of all, don't feel that you are stuck with a label simply because it was given to you by a school or diagnostician. There is no getting around the fact that misdiagnosis can be made, especially if testing is not extensive enough to pick up the differences between underachievement and true learning disabilities (see the explanation on Learning Disabilities for more on how a learning disability should be determined).

Another possibility is that he was labeled to qualify for a school program. While this may still leave you with a false label, it is hard to fault the school for trying to help a struggling student. Often, the only way to get children the help they need is to label them so that they can be put into special classes or programs.

The bottom line here is that if you bring home a child with a label, and you find that the label no longer "fits," that is fine. It probably wasn't the right diagnosis in the first place. You're not stuck with it. As I've said before, the label doesn't matter as much as what you do with the difficulties you have. If you had a false label, praise the Lord and move on!

RESOURCES
(unless otherwise noted, books are available on amazon.com)

Christian Home Educators Curriculum Manuals, Cathy Duffy and **100 Top Picks for Homeschool Curriculum: Choosing the Right Curriculum and Approach for Your Child's Learning Style** by Cathy Duffy
Cathy does a nice job of explaining learning styles. She goes beyond the typical auditory, visual, kinesthetic styles to give some unique insights into why children learn the way they do. Also see Cathy's website: http://cathyduffyreviews.com/

The Weaver Curriculum - Teaching Tips and Techniques, Rebecca Avery

A very thorough look at how children learn and what types of skills need to be present prior to formal learning. Lots of great activities for children slow in maturing who need work in "readiness." Available from Alpha Omega Publishers www.aop.com

Raising Your Spirited Child: A Guide for Parents Whose Child Is More, Mary Sheedy Kurcinka

I'm including this book because often children who are spirited or strong-willed can be confused with children with ADD or other learning problems. This book is not from a Christian perspective, so I didn't always agree with some of her views on discipline, but I did find many of her ideas (such as the use of humor) very refreshing.

CHAPTER 4

Learning Disabilities

THE TERM "LEARNING disabilities" encompasses a wide range of special-learning needs. In many ways these can be the most frustrating kinds of disabilities for both parents and children. Not only do we have a number of people declaring that these disabilities don't exist (tell that to the parents and students struggling with these difficulties!), but learning disabilities are often virtually invisible except during "school" activities. Because of this, many people do not understand the struggles that both parents and children encounter on a daily basis, and it is typical for these parents to feel unsupported and misunderstood within the home school community.

In order to have a learning disability, a person must demonstrate three things: average intelligence, below average achievement, and evidence of interference in receiving, processing, or reproducing information.

Let's look at these three criteria more closely. The first two are fairly easy to get a handle on. **Average Intelligence** means

17

that your child scores at least a 90 or above on a test of general intelligence (like the Broad Ability score on the Woodcock-Johnson or the Full Scale IQ on the WISC-R). I want to interject here that although scores above 90 are considered average, in my experience, children scoring in the low 90's usually learn at a bit slower pace and require more repetition than other "average" children. For these children, the definition and strategies for Slow Learners may be more appropriate.

Below Average Achievement is also fairly easy to understand. In fact, this is usually what sends parents looking for help in the first place. This is simply the fact that the child is achieving below his expected grade level on a test of standard achievement, such as the IOWA, SAT, etc.

It is when we start talking about **Evidence of Interference** to the learning process that things start to get interesting! The easiest way to understand this is to think of yourself as being able to do really only three things with information; you can **receive** it (take it in), you can **process** it (organize, store, and recall it), and you can **reproduce** it (get it out). You also have three systems that allow you to do these things. You can take in, process, and reproduce through your **Visual** system, your **Language** system, or your **Motor** system. One other system, your **Attention** system, either helps or further interferes with each of these areas.

Children with true learning disabilities demonstrate interference in one or more of these systems, which makes learning difficult. This is beyond a learning style or preference. These are real breakdowns that cause learning to be inefficient and often painful. The varieties of breakdowns are as varied as the children who have these difficulties, but let me give some examples of the more typical patterns of learning disabilities within each of the learning systems.

Visual System Disorders

Children with visual system difficulties have difficulty either taking in visual information, processing it, or reproducing it. These are the children who may see words or letters backwards when reading, or they may write their letters and words backwards when reproducing information. They may have difficulty with visual memory and so have difficulty remembering spelling patterns that are non-phonetic or other purely visual information. (By the way, these are the children whose reading problems generally can be helped with intensive phonics.)

Motor System Disorders

Children with motor system difficulties primarily have problems in the reproduction of information in writing. They may be able to give you a very detailed description of something orally, but with pencil in hand they look almost illiterate. Some of these children have difficulty with **motor memory,** which means that every time they begin to write a letter, they have to consciously think of how to form it. Thus, writing is a very painful and time-consuming prospect for these children.

Auditory System (Language) Disorders

Children with auditory difficulties often hear sounds in a distorted manner or have difficulty distinguishing between which of two sounds is most important (e.g., a bee buzzing or a person talking). These children have difficulty accurately remembering what they hear and may be confused by too much oral explanation. They are sometimes good sight readers and spellers if there is no visual system interference, but phonics often makes little sense to them. These children often misinterpret what is being said to them and are easily upset by noise. They may have difficulty with vocabulary and word meanings. Often they are very concrete learners who have difficulty with double meanings, inferences, and other language subtleties.

Attention System Disorders

First of all, we need to establish that children with Attention Deficit Disorder and Attention Deficit Hyperactive Disorder are not just wiggly little boys who need to get outside and run around more. This is a true physical interference of either the ability to attend efficiently or to break attention appropriately. Attention problems can really be some of the most difficult types of learning problems to cope with. The bottom line is that no matter how good your other systems may be, if you can't attend, you can't learn.

For some children, medication can be helpful in assisting them to focus and take in information more efficiently. However, medication is not always an answer, and many parents are reluctant to try it. If you do not want to try medication for an attention problem, some of the resources on allergies or sensory therapy may be avenues for you to pursue. I have seen success with a variety of approaches. Again, we must remember that each child is unique and you know your child best.

For those of you considering the use of medication, let me give you some general pros and cons. I should first say that I am not opposed to using medication, but neither do I think that it is a cure-all. For some children, medication can make focusing and attending possible where it was virtually impossible before, thus allowing learning to take place. So when the attention problem is quite severe and significantly interfering with most learning, I'm usually in favor of trying medication. I might also recommend trying medication for the child who is so overly focused as to be perseverative (unable to break focus on one item or thought). Sometimes this can be such a severe problem that it also prevents meaningful learning from taking place.

It is true that the use of medication can be abused. Medicating children who are capable of attending and learning without the medication would not be responsible. In the same way, using medication but failing to continue working on behavior, attention skills, etc., would be just as irresponsible. However, if medication is used responsibly and is well monitored by a knowledgeable doctor, it can often give you the edge in teaching coping and behavior skills where that was impossible before.

Most people I talk with are concerned over the safety of these medications. Obviously, the person to discuss this with is your doctor. It is sometimes difficult to determine exact dosages, and just getting a child regulated on a medication can be a time-consuming process. We tried several medications with our daughter for her attention and behavioral difficulties. After a lot of trial and error we found both the right medication and the proper dosage. We used this medication for about eighteen months and found that it helped her focus enough that I could teach her some of the attending and coping skills that I had previously been unable to work on with her. We eventually discontinued the use of the medication as we found supplements that worked for her. But this is certainly not the case for all children.

It is important to remember that we have to make decisions of this kind based on our own children and family situations, not what is popular or unpopular with other home school parents. There will always be people who oppose whatever we do. We must make our decisions based on our needs and the needs of our children and not the opinions of others. If you can cope with your child's level of attention or can find alternative treatments that you are more comfortable with, then don't let anyone pressure you into medication. The resource list at the end of this section has references for exploring alternative treatments for ADD. On the other hand, if you find medication helpful for your child, don't let others make you feel guilty for using it, either.

Remediation or Compensation?

One of the biggest debates in the field of Learning Disabilities is what we should do with these children! There are basically two "camps" here—those who believe in compensation and those who believe in remediation. I think it is important for home schooling parents to understand these two perspectives. Depending on the bias of the person evaluating your child or giving you program planning advice, you may get a very different picture of your child and the assumed needs that he has.

The idea behind compensation is to ignore, for the most part, the child's weak areas and to teach to his strengths. Proponents of this style of teaching argue that trying to remediate the underlying causes of learning disabilities is a poor use of time that could be used in teaching the child how to cope with or work around his learning problem. They also argue that we can't be sure that working on underlying skills, such as auditory memory, will really translate into gains in reading or language processing.

A typical compensation program might look something like this: let's say we have a ten-year-old girl who tests as having deficits in short-term memory, processing speed, and auditory processing. She works slowly and has difficulty with reading comprehension, math calculation, and spelling. Her mother has been using a phonics program for the past four years, along with a fairly traditional textbook approach. Planning a program from a purely compensation standpoint would emphasize her strong visual areas by suggesting that she be provided with picture cues for improving her reading comprehension, that she be taught to use a calculator for math and that she work on a computer with spell check when doing written work.

In contrast, a purely remedial program might begin by ignoring the academic difficulties in favor of working to improve memory and auditory processing skills first. This would be done with non-academic exercises, such as repeating sentences and numbers from memory. Phonics drills might be used to both remediate the spelling difficulties and strengthen the auditory system.

Which of these approaches is better? I feel that neither of them is completely on target. I prefer to mix compensation and remediation approaches in ways that seem both realistic and appropriate to each student. Younger children, especially, are good candidates for more remedial work on both underlying processes, such as memory and auditory skills, and basic academic skills. As children get older, however, I believe compensation-style programs become more realistic. Most of the time, I mix the two freely!

If I were planning a program for the girl from the earlier example, I would probably suggest that since phonics wasn't working, we set it aside for awhile and try to build reading comprehension using a more visual program (a compensation strategy). At the same time, I would suggest a dictation program for language arts that would emphasize accurate listening and proofreading to build both auditory memory and processing as well as to improve writing skills (remedial). Finally, I would probably suggest math drill exercises to strengthen her basic skills (remedial), but the use of a calculator during any other math work or during tests (compensation).

Another way to combine these approaches is to use a child's interests and strengths to build weak areas. For example, a friend of mine tells how they used her son's interest in carpentry to build up his weak math skills. Because it does make a difference if you cut the board 1/2 "wide, or 5/8" wide, fractions started to make sense! Using practical, meaningful learning experiences can make working on weak areas more palatable and successful. (See the chapter titled Choosing Teaching Methods and Techniques for more ideas on using interests.) So you see, we don't have to be locked into any one viewpoint. Make a program that fits your child's needs and that won't make everyone crazy at the same time! (We will discuss this more when we get to program planning.)

RESOURCES
(Unless otherwise noted, books are available on amazon.com)

There is a wealth of resources in the field of learning disabilities—in fact it is almost overwhelming. Unfortunately, they do not all agree with each other as to the best way to define or work with these children. I'm going to list just a few resources that I have used and found the most helpful.

Keeping A Head in School and **All Kinds of Minds**, Melvin D. Levine, M.D.

Both books are written for children to read themselves so they can understand about their learning abilities and learning disorders. A good intro for parents. www.avcsbooks.com

Developmental Variation and Learning Disorders, Melvin D. Levine, M.D.

I recommend anything Dr. Levine has written, but this book is the "classic." Simply everything you could ever want to know about learning disabilities! Takes a non-labeling approach, which I like. Lots of theory, but also many very practical management and teaching techniques. Available from Educators Publishing Service, 31 Smith Pl., Cambridge, MA 02138-1000 1.800.225.5750 www.epsbooks.com

http://www.allkindsofminds.org/ Dr. Mel Levine's website. Full of information and resources.

http://www.schwablearning.org/ Website originated by Charles Schwab to provide research, resources, and management strategies for parents of children with learning disabilities.

Learning in Spite of Labels, Joyce Herzog

This is a definite "must have" book if you are home schooling any children with learning disabilities. Joyce is a LD Specialist with over twenty-five years of experience and a heart for home schooling! Her teaching tips are right on, and her explanations are concise and understandable.

Overcoming Dyslexia, Sally Shaywitz, M.D.

This book offers one of the best and most comprehensive overviews of dyslexia I've seen. It will really help parents understand this disability. However, the author does not agree with parents teaching their children—so don't let that part throw you. The rest of the book is excellent.

Solving the Puzzle of Your Hard to Raise Child, William G. Crook, M.D.

This is an old book (1987), but for those of you who would like to explore the allergy-LD-ADD connection, I think this is one of the most balanced books on the subject. I found used copies on amazon, but you can also check the library.

Specific ADD Resources

Driven to Distraction, Edward M. Hallowell, M.D.

An excellent overview of ADD. It clearly explains what being ADD is like for a child and adult, the impact it has on families and schooling, and time/task management techniques that are effective for children and adults.

Healing ADD, Daniel G. Amen

Although I don't really like the title of this book, you may or may not be able to actually "heal" ADD, it is the best book I know for breaking down the six types of ADD and offering specific, practical ideas for treatment and management.

Therapies

Three of the most common therapy approaches used with learning-disabled children are the Orton-Gillingham/Slingerland approach, the deficit remediation therapy used by the National Institute for Learning Disabilities, and the Lindamood-Bell approach. These therapies are all effective, but very expensive and time-consuming (often taking three years or more for results). Of the three, I think the Lindamood-Bell program is the most comprehensive and effective.

Other helpful therapies include vision therapy (for those with visual perception issues), biofeedback therapy (used mostly with ADD students), and sensory integration therapy (useful for ADD issues as well as motor and sensory issues).

For more information on these approaches or the availability of therapists in your area, contact the following:

Lindamood-Bell Clinics www.lblp.com
Explanation of the program, list of clinics, many of the program materials available for purchase.

The Lindamood-Bell manuals and workbooks are also available for parents to purchase on our website (www.avcsbooks.com) if you want to work on this approach at home. See the reviews under reading, language, and math for **Seeing Stars** (phonics and spelling), **Visualizing and Verbalizing** (language and comprehension), and **On Cloud Nine** (math) in Section Three.

The International Dyslexia Association http://www.interdys. org/
Learn about Orton-Gillingham therapy and search for a dyslexia therapist or program.

We carry many phonics materials that follow the Orton-Gillingham approach advocated by IDA. See the reviews in Section Three or visit our website at www.avcsbooks.com for **Recipe for Reading,**

Explode the Code, Primary Phonics, How to Teach Spelling and Megawords.

Barton Reading Program 408.559.3652 www.bartonreading.com

A tutoring system for dyslexia and learning disabilities. Program includes videos and workbooks. Expensive, but effective if you stick with it.

Language Tune-Up Kit www.jwor.com

Another Orton-Gillingham based tool—this one for the computer. Much more affordable. My son found it "boring" but it is effective.

National Institute for Learning Development http://www.nild.net

Learn about the NILD therapy model and search for programs in your area.

College of Optometrists in Vision Development http://www.covd.org/

Learn about vision therapy and find a doctor in your area.

How to Teach Your Child to Read and Spell Successfully, Sheldon Rappaport

This book explains visual perception disabilities and gives specific exercises that can be done at home to enhance these functions. Available from www.avcsbooks.com.

EEG Spectrum International 818.789.3456 http://www.eegspectrum.com/

Information on neurofeedback and to find a provider

Sensory Integration and the Young Child, Jean Ayres

The original book about sensory integration therapy and its benefits.

The Out-of-Sync Child, Carol Stock Kranowitz
A wonderful resource for information and practical ways to enhance the lives of children with sensory integration disorder.

If you would like to explore diet and supplements that may help ADD or other learning issues, check out www.diannecraft.com.

CHAPTER 5

Slow Learners

A SLOW LEARNER IS a child who falls in between the criteria for learning disabilities and mental retardation. This is the child who scores in the 70-90 IQ range in tests of general intelligence but does not show the high and low score pattern associated with the interferences of a true learning disability. That is, she is capable of learning, but it is as if everything is just turned down a notch. These children typically work two to three or more grade levels below their age group. They require a lot of repetition in order to retain information but usually do retain it once it is learned well.

Typically, when one of these children is tested in the school systems, parents are told that the child is "working up to his potential" and therefore does not quality for special help. But these children are often so far behind their peers that school becomes meaningless, and they are most at risk for dropping out of school as soon as they are of age to do so.

These children will absolutely, positively benefit from home schooling, but only as long as the parents recognize the learning problem and are willing to give the children the repetition and allow them to move at the slow pace they need.

Unfortunately, I have not seen any specific resources addressing the slow learner. I think that the best thing parents of these children can do is to forget grade levels and get some good academic testing to pinpoint were the child is functioning. Then move forward at the pace the child can handle. Be prepared to teach concepts several times and in several different ways. Repetition and variety are the key words! In my experience, slow learners are the ones who most like to work in textbooks or workbooks and often do best with very simplified, step-by-step curriculum that sticks with the basics. Some comprehensive curriculums that have been particularly helpful to families I have worked with are listed below. Other ideas will be found in the curriculum section. One thing to keep in mind is that you can really use just about anything with a slow learner that you can use with children without learning problems; you just need to move to the appropriate level and work at an overall slower pace.

RESOURCES

Many of the books listed under learning disabilities will still be appropriate for parents of slow learners. I would especially recommend Joyce Herzog's book, *Learning in Spite of Labels*, because her "25 Teaching Techniques that Work" give some excellent ideas and reminders for all struggling students.

Comprehensive Curriculums

LIFEPACS and Switched on Schoolhouse, Alpha Omega Publications

A standard curriculum that comes in small workbooks instead of large textbooks. Some students seem to be less overwhelmed by the smaller amount of work in each workbook rather than looking at a textbook and being discouraged if they can't complete it in a year. Switched on Schoolhouse is the computer option. Available from Alpha Omega Publications, P. O. Box 3153, Tempe, AZ 85280 1.800.622.3070 (orders), 1.800.821.4443 (information) www.aop.com

School of Tomorrow

This curriculum is also a workbook series similar to the LIFEPACS. Available from ACE School of Tomorrow, P. O. Box 1438, Lewisville, TX 750647-1438 1.800.925.7777 www.schooloftomorrow.com

www.time4learning.com

This is a computer based curriculum that can be used as an entire curriculum or just for one or two subjects. We have found that many students are able to be more independent on the computer which really boosts their confidence.

CHAPTER 6

Language and Communication Disorders

THE BIGGEST QUESTION here is what separates a Language/Communication Disorder from a Language Learning Disability. The answer is severity and age of onset. Children who demonstrate Language or Communication Disorders do so at young ages. We usually spot these children at the age of two or three when they fail to develop speech and language skills at the expected rate or age levels. These children generally have difficulties with speech articulation, comprehension of spoken language, or language expression. Many children have difficulty in all three of these areas to one extent or another.

Typically, they also demonstrate behavior difficulties because of frustration in their attempts to communicate or lack of understanding of what is expected of them. In testing, many of these children demonstrate a depressed IQ score, but this is usually due to their very low scores in any area dealing with language. When given nonverbal tests of intelligence, such as the Leiter, these children can perform in the normal range.

A typical child with a Language/Communication Disorder may look something like this: he may appear bright and reach all of his motor milestones on time, but he may not begin talking until two or three, and may have a few words compared with children of his age. The words he has may be difficult to understand. He often has temper tantrums or fails to respond to discipline because he lacks understanding of the demands being placed on him. He may begin speaking in sentences but will confuse pronouns ("Her is eating") and often does not call himself by name or use appropriate pronouns for himself.

In my experience, most pediatricians will take a "wait and see" attitude with these children, often telling harried mothers that this is something he will "grow out of." But the fact is that unless this is only a mild speech difficulty, most children do not grow out of these problems, and without some intervention the child's frustration and behavior problems continue to worsen.

If you have a child who appears to fall into this category, I believe it is wise to consult a speech and language therapist. While you may want to work with your child yourself at home, it is often difficult to pinpoint where to start working although some of the resources listed below may help. If articulation is the only difficulty, check out Marisa Lapish's program, Straight Talk (www.nathhan.com). Her program teaches you how to evaluate and remediate speech difficulties.

Deafness

Deafness is considered a Language/Communication disorder, but obviously has some special issues. Deciding what communication system to use can be a difficult, emotional, and confusing process. One good resource to begin with is the book **Choices in Deafness: A Parent's Guide to Communication Options,** by Sue Schwartz. I really liked the tone of this book. It presents all of the various communication options as well as stories from families explaining why they chose the approach they did and how it has worked for them.

Most deaf students do not need specialized curriculum except when it comes to teaching reading. I recommend the **Reading Milestones** (www.avcsbooks.com) curriculum for teaching reading not only to deaf children, but to any child with a severe language disorder.

RESOURCES

A Metacognitive Program for Treating Auditory Processing Disorders, Patricia McAleer Hamaguchi

Learn how to teach metacognitive (thinking) strategies to children who have an auditory processing disorder with this thorough book. The strategies are taught in a hierarchical order so that students are able to grasp and build upon skills that will help them to better listen to and comprehend orally presented material. (www.avcsbooks.com)

"Talkies" Teacher's Manual

This program is a simplified version of the Lindamood-Bell Visualizing and Verbalizing program. It is aimed at younger or more severely language disabled students. Multisensory, step-by-step format will help develop oral language comprehension, and expression. (www.avcsbooks.com)

Listen My Children and You Shall Hear

Levels: Preschool– Grade 4 *New Expanded Version*

Appropriate for: Children who have auditory processing difficulties

This book is described by the author as "a manual of stories and exercises designed to help children develop listening skills, auditory memory, vocabulary, and imagination." I used this book when I was doing educational therapy, and found it extremely helpful. (www. avcsbooks.com)

Catalogs & Websites

LinguiSystems, 1.800.776.4332. www.linguisystems.com
This catalog is jam-packed with resources for working with children with language and communication difficulties. All of their products are top-notch, and they are very helpful in answering questions when you call.

Enabling Devices www.enablingdevices.com
Carries a huge variety of communicators for non-verbal and speech impaired people.

Mayer-Johnson (www.mayer-johnson.com) 800-588-4548
Creators of the PECS (Picture Exchange Communication System). They also carry some curriculum materials that use the picture symbols.

Pro-Ed, 512.451.8542. www.proedinc.com
Pro-Ed carries a large selection of books on Language and Communication Disorders. Although they are mostly addressed to clinicians, they are good resources for learning more about these disorders. They also carry many curriculum products for working with language difficulties.

If you are looking for a qualified audiologist or speech-language pathologist in your area, contact the American Speech-Language-Hearing Association (www.asha.org). They also have many brochures available on recognizing and understanding speech and communication disorders.

CHAPTER 7

Mental Retardation (Developmental Disabilities)

CHILDREN THAT DEMONSTRATE mental retardation are a large and varied group! Generally, two criteria must be met in order for a child to be considered retarded. He must score below 69 on a test of general intelligence, and he must demonstrate difficulty with adaptive behavior. Adaptive behavior refers to functional daily living skills such as communication, self-help skills, social skills, and sensory skills. Another way to say this is that retarded children have both difficulties in learning and in coping with the world around them. Although this statement could be said to be true of many learning-disabled, language-disordered, and slow-learning children also, it is the degree of difficulty that distinguishes the mentally retarded child from children with these other disabilities.

Still, sometimes it is difficult to distinguish the severely language-disordered child from the very mildly retarded child. This is why it is again not important to get hung up on labels but on what interventions are necessary for this child to reach his full potential.

For most of you with children falling in this category, you either knew right away that your child had a disability (e.g., if your child has Down Syndrome) or it was obvious at a fairly young age that your child was not developing at a normal rate. You have probably been "home schooling" for as long as you remember, since these children need specific instruction in almost every area of skill acquisition and development.

In my consulting, I have found that parents with developmentally disabled children are usually fairly well informed about their children's disabilities, but don't feel confident in their ability to teach them. Because many of your children have been in early intervention programs or are receiving various forms of therapy, you may have the feeling that you are not qualified to take on the task of schooling, but I believe that you are. I want to encourage you to read the next section of this book, "Tackling the Issues," which I hope will encourage you that you are capable of teaching your child!

In general, children with retardation learn at a significantly slower rate than other children and need constant repetition to maintain skills (although some children resist review, and materials have to be varied in order to maintain interest). Most developmentally disabled children I have worked with do best when activities are related to real life situations since adaptive skills are also weak. So, for example, it would be more beneficial for children to count forks while learning to set the table than counting blocks, because you are not only teaching counting but also stressing practical skills.

Although many Down Syndrome children can learn basic phonics, the majority of children with retardation learn to read by sight. It is often helpful to have them learn sign language as a means of adding a kinesthetic element to reading. For more ideas on curriculum and teaching methods, please see those sections.

RESOURCES

There are many good, general resources on mental retardation available. Here are a couple of good ones to start with.

Children with Mental Retardation, edited by Romayne Smith
This book was recommended by one of the mothers in my group. She said it had a lot of good information for someone just getting "hit" with a diagnosis of retardation and an especially good chapter on dealing with your emotions.

Individualized Assessment and Treatment for Autistic and Developmentally Disabled Children Vol II, Teaching Strategies for Parents and Professionals, Schopler, Reichler, and Lansing
This is an excellent book that gives you very helpful information on how children with developmental disabilities learn, as well as practical goals, objectives, teaching strategies and behavior-management techniques. www.avcsbooks.com

Teaching Activities for Autistic (and Developmentally Delayed) Children
Companion volume to the above book, this is a comprehensive guide to planning programs for severely disabled children. Contains

activities in imitation, perception, gross motor, fine motor, eye-hand integration, cognitive performance, cognitive verbal, self-help, and social areas. Also contains a very helpful developmental level chart to help you determine your child's functional age in each category. The directions for the activities tend to be very "behavior modification" oriented which turns some people off, but I have used this extensively as a guide and idea resource even though I use a more "environmental" approach to teaching my daughter. www.avcsbooks.com

Teaching Reading to Children with Down Syndrome, Patricia Logan Oelwein www.avcsbooks.com

This book provides an excellent method for teaching sight reading to any severely handicapped child. Combine it with the Reading Milestones readers (www.avcsbooks.com) for a complete sight reading program. This author has several other books dealing with various aspects of teaching children with mental retardation. Check amazon.com for other titles.

Love and Learning www.loveandlearning.com

A reading program developed especially for children with Down Syndrome. Uses video presentations and readers to develop basic reading and language skills.

Catalogs

Pro-Ed www.proedinc.com

Pro-Ed carries a fairly large selection of books and curriculum materials for mental retardation.

Edmark www.edmark.com

A major supplier of materials for developmentally disabled students. They especially have a great selection of computer software and adaptive tools for the computer.

CHAPTER 8

Autism Spectrum Disorders

Autism (Low-Functioning)

ALTHOUGH THERE IS much debate regarding the cause, I think everyone who works with an autistic child would agree that it is one of the most challenging learning handicaps. Autistic children demonstrate severe difficulty with language and communication, behavior, sensory response, social skills, and motor skills. Low-functioning autistic children fall into the mentally retarded range of intellectual functioning. I often say that it is every learning difficulty you can think of wrapped into one package!

Additionally, autistic children often relate to people and objects in abnormal ways, which can make teaching very difficult. Some autistic children have extreme behaviors, such as self-injury, aggression, or repetitive behaviors that require management over and above any skill or academic concerns.

Teaching a child with autism is a painfully slow process. Many autistic children (approximately fifty percent) are non-verbal, so teaching must encompass alternative communication methods as well as other skills. Some children are capable of signing, and some have been more successful with augmentative systems, such as picture boards (we used both, and my daughter has done better with sign and written words, although I often used pictures to introduce new words). Typing is also a potential communication tool if the fine motor skills are there and the child is capable of learning to read. Some families have used facilitated communication as a means of communication where another person supports the hand of the autistic person so they can type. There is some controversy with this technique, and I think it is always best to try and work on independent typing as much as possible. If you have a good facilitator who doesn't try and "help" with the content, it can be a good technique for the higher functioning, non-verbal student.

Because autistic children resist change, and anything new is seen as a threat, teaching situations and materials must be changed periodically, or the child will not be able to generalize learning to other situations. For example, my daughter learned to count using a certain book with clowns in it, but when I wanted to transfer that skill to counting on the computer program, she screamed bloody murder and seemed to have "forgotten" how to count!

I think that with children who have severe difficulties, such as autism, it is very important that we keep sight of the "Big Picture" and not lose heart. Every little bit of progress needs to be celebrated and seen as significant, and we need to keep plugging away!

Autism (High-Functioning)

The biggest difference between high-functioning autism and low-functioning autism is the intellectual potential. High-functioning autistic people have average intelligence, but display the same language, communication, social, and behavioral issues as low-functioning individuals. High-functioning autistic children often excel at specific rote academic tasks, but have difficulty with reasoning skills and comprehension skills beyond the fact level.

Asperger Syndrome

Asperger Syndrome is characterized by high intelligence along with many of the sensory, coping, and behavior difficulties normally associated with autism. Children with AS have extreme difficulty with change or disruption to routine. They often become obsessed with a particular topic and have difficulty relating to anything else. They tend to have difficulty with language beyond the literal level and are very concrete thinkers who get particularly upset by being asked to use figurative language or imagination. One AS boy I worked with was particularly distressed at being given an assignment to "Describe what might have happened if Abraham Lincoln had not been assassinated," because—as he said so emphatically—"They did shoot him. That's the fact. How can they think I can lie about that?" Social skills are especially difficult for these children because they are not interested in other people and do not have an understanding of other people's perspective.

These can be particularly challenging children to work with and live with because their intelligence is so obvious, but their common sense and ability to deal with the world around them functionally is so poor.

Non-Verbal Learning Disorders

Although some people do not classify NLD as an Autism Spectrum Disorder, I think it fits best here. Non-Verbal Learning Disorder encompasses children whose visual learning disabilities are extreme. These children often have excellent verbal skills, but their language is very literal and their ability to use the visual clues of the environment is almost nonexistent. While children with NLD share many characteristics with the Asperger Syndrome student described above, the main difference is that while AS children have difficulty with social interaction because of their peculiar and narrow interests, the child with NLD has trouble with social interaction because he just doesn't "get" any of the non-literal language or visual cues (facial expressions, body language, etc.) used in social interaction. Additionally, these children tend to have more academic difficulty and demonstrate more motor issues than most AS kids.

A good resource on NLD is *The Source for Non-Verbal Learning Disorders* by Sue Thompson available from LinguiSystems www. linguisystems.com.

RESOURCES

Children with Autism, edited by Michael Powers, Psy.D. This is an old book, but it was the first one I read after my daughter's diagnosis, and I think it still is a great resource for someone just starting out. It has many quotes from parents, and they really helped me feel like I wasn't alone as I adjusted to the diagnosis.

Individualized Assessment and Treatment for Autistic and Developmentally Disabled Children Vol II, Teaching Strategies for Parents and Professionals, Schopler, Reichler, and Lansing

This is an excellent book that gives you very helpful information on how children with developmental disabilities learn, as well as practical goals, objectives, teaching strategies, and behavior-management techniques. www.avcsbooks.com

Teaching Activities for Autistic (and Developmentally Delayed) Children

Companion volume to the above book, this is a comprehensive guide to planning programs for severely disabled children. Contains activities in imitation, perception, gross motor, fine motor, eye-hand integration, cognitive performance, cognitive verbal, self-help, and social areas. Also contains a very helpful developmental level chart to help you determine your child's functional age in each category. The directions for the activities tend to be very "behavior modification" oriented which turns some people off, but I have used this extensively as a guide and idea resource even though I use a more "environmental" approach to teaching my daughter. www.avcsbooks.com

Sensory Integration and the Young Child, Jane Ayres

Sensory Integration therapy can be very helpful for children who are over-sensitive to environmental stimuli, such as touch, and who have balance and motor-system difficulties that interfere with attention and learning. My daughter had extensive SI therapy and we found it very helpful.

The Sound of a Miracle, Anabel Stehli

Details the author's experience with Auditory Enhancement Training and how it cured her daughter of autism. Although I get tired of these "miracle" books, it did prompt me to research AET, which we did end up doing twice. It proved helpful for my daughter, although it was not a cure.

Emergence: Labeled Autistic, Temple Grandin, PhD

Thinking in Pictures, Temple Grandin, PhD
I found these accounts by a (very high functioning) autistic person very helpful in understanding some of my daughter's behaviors (especially her sensitivity to touch).

Mayer-Johnson (www.mayer-johnson.com) 800-588-4548
Creators of the PECS (Picture Exchange Communication System). They also carry some curriculum materials that use the picture symbols.

Autism Research Institute http://www.autism.com/
Information on the latest treatments for autism.

Asperger Syndrome by Tony Atwood
The leading expert on AS. Very well written and informative.

OASIS (Online Asperger Syndrome Information and Support) http://www.udel.edu/bkirby/asperger/
Start here. Everything you ever need to know and a great resource section.

Curriculum

(More curriculum will be found at the end of the book, but I will highlight a few things here that are specific to the Autism Disorders).

Navigating the Social World, *Jeanette McAfee, M.D.*

A curriculum for individuals with Asperger Syndrome, High-Functioning Autism, and related disorders. This important new book offers a definitive program with forms, exercises, and guides for the student. It also presents significant educational guidance and supportive ideas for parents. www.avcsbooks.com

Reading Milestones

This is a sight reading program designed for deaf, developmentally disabled or any other children with severe auditory disabilities. As with any sight program, long-term memory needs to be a relative strength for the child; however, the workbooks do provide some practice in word analysis skills as well as practice in sequencing and comprehension. This is the program I used with my autistic, mentally retarded daughter. The books have delightful illustrations, but there are several stories that deal with dressing up for Halloween as ghosts and witches and these have bothered some of the parents I have shown this program to. I would say that if those stories bother you, skip them, but if you have a child who needs a sight approach to reading, this is definitely the one I would choose. www.avcsbooks.com

Apple Tree Language Program

A structured, sequential approach to developing good sentence structure as the basis for written language skills. Aimed at children with language processing disorders (such as autism) who are reading at approximately a second grade level. I like the many pictures and charts used throughout this program which help clarify structures that children with language problems find confusing. www.avcsbooks.com

"Talkies" Teacher's Manual

This program is a simplified version of the Lindamood-Bell "Visualizing and Verbalizing" program. It is aimed at younger or more severely language disabled students such as those with autism. Multisensory, step-by-step format will help develop oral language comprehension and expression. www.avcsbooks.com

GENERAL RESOURCES
(ALL DISABILITIES)

NATHHAN (National Challenged Homeschoolers Associated Network) www.nathhan.com or (208) 267-6246

Articles, support group listings, newsletter, lending library, resource lists, and some curriculum.

Home School Legal Defense Association

If you are not already a member of HSLDA you should be. It is wise for all home schoolers to belong to HSLDA, but it is even more prudent for those of us with special needs children. Not only do they provide legal covering, but they have a Special Needs Coordinator who maintains a data base of special education consultants throughout the United States. P. O. Box 159, Paeonian Springs, VA 22129 703.338.5600, or www. hslda.org

Section Two
Tackling the Issues

Now that we've established some basic knowledge, we need to turn to the issues of home schooling a special needs child. Almost everyone I work with wants to know first which books or curriculum they should use. In dealing with our special children, I actually see this as the *least* important issue to deal with. I believe that in order to effectively teach our special needs children, we first must deal with two main issues that can create roadblocks to our effectiveness—our expectations and our emotions.

While the special needs of our children may be quite different, in our school and support group we have found that the issues affecting us (as teaching moms of disabled children) are the same, regardless of our children's difficulties. Some of the issues that we must deal with involve the emotions of parenting and teaching a child with a learning difficulty. Some issues concern the way we see our children, and some concern the way we react to other people's perception of us. I believe that until we work through these issues, our teaching will not be as effective as possible.

We are going to look at some of the most typical issues that are roadblocks to effective home schooling. Some may apply to you more directly than others, or some may apply to you differently at different times. They are, however, all things we need to acknowledge if we are to successfully home school our special children.

CHAPTER 9

Realistic Expectations for Home Schooling

ONE OF THE very first things that we need to deal with is having a realistic view of what home schooling can and cannot do for our special needs children. Home schooling is not a magic cure for any of our children's learning or behavior problems. Many of the parents that I work with are very disappointed that after bringing a child home from school they don't just "shed" all of their learning difficulties and make tremendous strides academically. Of course, as I mentioned before, we have all heard about those children who were labeled in the school system, and who came home and just "took off" without any more learning problems. It does happen; it's just that those children are not disabled. They are the "mis-matched" children I talked about in the first section—the children who didn't "fit" the education system in some critical way and ended up inappropriately labeled ADD or LD.

However, if you are bringing home (or have at home) a child with a true disability, that disability will not go away with home schooling. (By the way, it also won't go away with more love, or more discipline, or less discipline, or unschooling, or any of the other things I hear that have been advised by "regular" home schoolers.)

So, if home schooling can't cure our children's disabilities, what can home schooling do? The first and most important thing that home schooling gives our children is us. These are the children who, more than most others, need a safe place to learn and grow in their own way and at their own pace. Other teachers may like or even love our children, but often we are the only ones who see the true potential of our children underneath their difficulties. That is because we are able to see our children as whole people, not just as a "disabilities." All children need people who love and believe in them, but children with learning and behavior difficulties are sometimes hard to love and believe in. They need the additional support and encouragement that we as parents can offer through home schooling.

An Individualized Program

The second thing that home schooling can do is to provide our children with truly individualized educational programs. Of course, the goal of any special education program, public or private, is to provide individualized programs for special needs students. But the fact is these programs still contain twelve to fourteen children in each classroom, many with distinctly different needs. Now, I am not a school basher by any stretch of the imagination. I know many gifted teachers who are working very hard to provide the best programs they possibly can for each and every student. But I also know from my own classroom experience that when we have a wide variety of needs in one room, we cannot adequately address each child's every need. Most things must be done in groups because there just aren't enough hours in the day to work one-on-one for any length of time. Programs that do provide more extensive one-on-one teaching are usually private and can be prohibitively expensive.

At home, however, we can truly individualize our children's programs. If they need a math book at one grade level, reading material at another level, and work in written language at still a third level, no sweat! We don't have a set curriculum that must be followed; we can pick and choose the right materials for our children at the right time.

One-on-One Teaching

The third thing that home schooling provides is real one-on-one teaching. My daughter was in a classroom for the severely handicapped for three years before we made the decision to bring her home. In that time, they worked on all the typical readiness activities, both in group settings and by giving some individual time to each child each week. If I had to rate the quality of the program she was in, I would say it was a seven on a scale of ten. Not bad. So why, after three years in this program, had she not made any real gains in basic readiness skills and was only able to truly demonstrate what she knew on the days I worked in her classroom? Why was it that after we brought her home, she learned her colors, numbers, letters, and how to cut (skills that had been worked on for the last three years with little progress) within a year and was reading simple three-word sentences within eighteen months? It is not because I am a miracle worker, and it is not because I am a perfect, loving mother (far, far from it). I believe it is because she got the one-on-one attention she needed and because I was willing to work through all of the resistance and behavior difficulties that, in reality, they just don't have time to do in a classroom of twelve children.

For example, I once observed a teacher attempting to teach my daughter to cut. She very patiently tried to put the scissors into Alison's hands, but Alison jerked away and screamed because she is very overly sensitive to touch. The teacher tried again and held the scissors with Alison, but Alison continued to scream and protest. The teacher said, "I guess Alison is not ready to do this," and sent her back to the group activity (which was what she wanted in the first place)—her one-on-one time was over for the day!

In contrast, I had both more time and more emotional investment in my daughter's progress. When we began working on cutting, I first did some tactile massage so that she wasn't so resistant to the feel of the scissors or my hands guiding her. When she screamed and tried to leave the activity, I told her that she didn't get to quit because she screamed, and that we had all day to work on this if necessary. Then we began working through the various aspects of cutting, step by step. In working with her, I discovered that her muscle tone was very poor. She could barely even hold onto the scissors by herself, so we worked on hand and finger strength as part of our overall program. The point is that because I was able to work one-on-one with her for the time she needed in order to work through her resistance and behavior difficulties, I was finally able to see what she needed to learn this skill, and we were able to make progress. In the classroom, her resistance would usually take so long that her individual time was up before much actual work could be done.

Even children who are not as disabled as my child do not get the one-on-one attention they need in a classroom setting. Often children with learning problems can be overly passive. They will sit and draw or daydream, but if they are not disruptive to the overall classroom, they may not be approached for individual help by the teacher or aide. Since they don't ask for help, they don't make much progress. If you think I'm exaggerating, I've seen it happen! Sometimes, an alert teacher will try to give time to these very passive children, but, again, that teacher only has so much time and a limited emotional investment in each child, so after awhile these children are just pretty much left alone.

"Full-Inclusion"

Another thing that home schooling accomplishes is that our children are "fully included." Full inclusion is a big buzz word in special education, and it basically aims at putting special education children into regular classrooms (usually with aides) so that they will not be segregated from "normal" children. The philosophy is that the special needs children will have better role models, and the "normal" children will learn tolerance and compassion for people with differences. This all sounds great, but can you imagine the typical schoolteacher who already has thirty children in her classroom, all at varying degrees of achievement within the "norm," adding in a child with mental retardation or autism or even just a communication disability? For most teachers this thought is overwhelming.

But think about what we offer our special needs children when they are at home—the best of both worlds! What could be more inclusive than a family? If you have several children, your special needs child is being provided with the good role

61

models and stimulation that is supposed to make full inclusion the better alternative, but he can still get the individual attention from you that he needs.

Of course, it can be a juggling act to give the attention needed to your special child and keep everyone else on track too. But our children all need to learn coping skills, and home schooling with a special needs child presents plenty of opportunities for learning coping skills and developing character! And it is not just the character of our children that is being built, but ours as well. I sometimes think that God has taught me more through my years of home schooling than I ever taught my children. On those really bad days, try thinking of all the character that is being built through your home school!

CHAPTER 10

Feeling Inadequate

SO MANY PEOPLE who want to teach their disabled children at home are afraid they will not be able to do a good job. Another issue we need to address in order to successfully teach our children is this feeling of inadequacy. It is not enough to believe that home schooling is a good alternative for our children if we don't have confidence in our ability to teach them. Of course, it is hard work and at times very frustrating, but unless we believe that we have the calling and capability to teach our children, we will spin our wheels in self-doubt and worry, both of which are very unproductive.

The "Experts" Say You Can't

Many of you may feel that you are not capable because you have been told so, point-blank, by an "expert" in the field of your child's disability. I talk to many people who have gone for assessments at clinics or special schools and have received appalled responses from the clinician or doctor when home schooling is mentioned. Responses such as this from professionals make it easy to doubt that you are doing the right thing. In working with the families in my program, I have come to see this as a critical issue that must be dealt with before much successful teaching can take place.

I think that it is important to understand why so many people in the education field strongly believe that parents should not teach their own children. I have to admit that I used to be one of those teachers who was appalled by the idea of home schooling a disabled child. After all, I had gone to school for special training in teaching these children. Also, many of the children I worked with drained me emotionally because of their resistance and other emotional problems, and some of these children I just plainly didn't like. How, I reasoned, could a mother deal with this kind of behavior with no special training and still push the child firmly and patiently through the things that were difficult for the child? Wouldn't these mothers, I thought, tend to baby the child and do things for the child that would result in more harm than good?

I have since come to see that often the opposite is true. Because of many factors, home school moms can be harder on their children and push them more than any teacher ever would. In my program, I have often counseled parents to relax and try to enjoy teaching their children because it is already hard enough without them making it harder! I have worked with many parents who were initially shocked that I was pleased with six months of growth in one year. But when I explain that the average child should grow one year in one year, they often realize that, yes, they are doing a good job!

Of course, I have seen parents who do too much for their children, but I have found that ninety-nine percent of the people I work with are open to ideas and learning better ways to teach their children. Having worked with many home school families for almost twenty years has only made me feel more convinced that these parents are not only capable of teaching their special needs children but are often doing a better job than that which I have seen in many schools.

Many professionals also see parents as ineffective in dealing with their children's behavior problems and reason that this will carry over into schooling. Actually, on this point I agree. If we cannot deal with our children's behavior, we cannot teach them anything. I believe strongly that our children's disabilities should never exempt them from being required to behave in an acceptable manner. They must learn obedience, respect for authority, and self-control just like any of our other children. (I will deal more with behavior later.)

However, we do need to also acknowledge that many children with learning problems have extreme behaviors that are harder to deal with than normal childish disobedience. This does not mean that these behaviors are the parents' fault, but unless we deal with them as best as possible, we are setting ourselves up for added stress in attempting to teach our children. Our children's extreme behavior is often the hardest part of their disabilities to accept. Children who are hyperactive, unfocused, resistant, impulsive, or immature are often hard to like, even when they are our children. There have been many days over the years that I have been wearied and discouraged by my daughter's behavior. These are issues that must be dealt with honestly if we are to be effective educators. (More on both of these issues to come!)

Other mothers that I speak with feel inadequate because they believe in their heart of hearts that their children must be missing something by not being in school, or they fear that there must be something that a specialist could do for their children that they can't. Most often these are the parents who have either never had their children in a school (if they had, they would know there is nothing magic happening there!); or they are parents who are home schooling because they feel they have no choice, but they have never really believed that it is the best answer for their children. The only thing I can really say is that if this is a major worry to you, a good consultant (who understands home schooling) can be an invaluable support. At this point, I'd like to let one of the mothers from my school explain how consulting has helped her feel more relaxed and adequate as a teacher for her daughter.

THE BENEFITS OF OBTAINING
A CONSULTANT

by Kathy Johnstone

My daughter, Kara, is seven years old and has a mild degree of mental retardation. Prior to meeting Sharon, she received speech and occupational therapy for three years as well as spending a year in a developmental pre-school. These specialists gave us ideas to implement, which provided the base for our home school program. Kara did progress slowly, but somehow I was always made to feel that Kara's problems or lack of progress were the result of our home schooling. I wanted to continue teaching her at home, but I felt like I needed some professional, yet pro-home school advice.

Having a consultant has relieved a great deal of stress for me. After going over results from testing, Sharon and I met to set up an IEP for the first quarter. We set specific goals to work toward in five different academic and non-academic areas and discussed how to meet those goals. It relieved me to have a specialist setting the goals, as she had Kara's total development in mind, and yet these goals were attainable! Sharon also gave me some books to read to educate myself. I was so relieved to realize that I did not have to work on every area simultaneously! The feelings of "never doing quite enough" began to disappear.

As Kara and I tackled these goals, we began to see more focused progress. By the end of the year, she had made some progress in every area. Although her scores weren't high, she was doing well, relative to children with her disability.

As you can see, Kathy has been a perfectly adequate teacher for her daughter, but she had been made to feel otherwise by professionals who didn't understand home schooling. This is not their fault, by the way, but it does remind us that if we are going to get consulting from someone, we must make sure they are pro-home schooling. Home School Legal Defense maintains a data base of special education consultants throughout the United States who are at best home schoolers themselves, but are, at the least, "home school friendly." This list can be obtained from the Special Needs Consultant at HSLDA if you are a member.

Pressure from Others

Others of you may feel inadequate because of pressure from family or friends to be miracle workers. I remember that when we first took Alison out of school, and for months afterwards, friends would come up to me and ask, "Well, how is she doing?" as if they expected that I had solved all her learning problems in the time we had been working at home. At first it made me feel defensive, but eventually I was able to just smile and say "Oh, we're plodding along!"

As I've said before, our society is obsessed with normal and even above normal. We must let go of the feelings that our children are less as people if they don't measure up academically, but we often have to educate those around us too. I have had many people come to me for consultation who were doing a perfectly great job teaching their children but were getting pressure from their husbands or other family members that, if home school were "working," the children should be up to grade level. If you are being pressured for results, do your best to educate that person about the learning problem your child has and what are realistic expectations for that child. Make sure you do have some support from either friends or other home schoolers with disabled children. And hang in there!

Why You Are Capable

So then, why do I believe that we are capable of teaching our special needs children? As I mentioned before, I believe it boils down to one thing—our love and belief in our children. Now I want to be careful here because I am not saying that I think that just by giving our children more love we will solve their learning problems. No, far from it. I know from personal experience that we are already giving our children all the love and support there is to give—we don't have any more! But it is that very belief in our child that will keep us going despite the frustrations and difficulties inherent to teaching special children.

Let me give an example that really brought this home to me. When I was working on my Special Education Master's, I had to put in a variety of different practicum hours. One of the field studies that was required was working at a camp for developmentally disabled children. I was assigned to work with a boy who was autistic. This little boy (who was about eight at the time) wore me out! He would take off unexpectedly, and I was constantly afraid that I would lose him or that he would get hurt. Once, he bolted away from me during a group time, raced across the camp yard and climbed a six foot chain link fence into the pool area, while I, in hot pursuit, screamed for someone to bring the key to the pool gate! It didn't take long before I dreaded the sight of this child each morning. Although I tried to help him participate in the programs as best I could, his behavior difficulties made it so that I often just gave up and let him sit. After all, I figured, he wasn't getting hurt if we just sat and watched the rest of the children participate in the activity! I didn't have any emotional stake in this child's having a successful camp experience or not. I felt more like I was just out to survive the time I had to put in. After the camp was over, and I had somewhat recovered from the physical and mental exhaustion, I remember thinking, "How do people cope with children like that? I'm sure I could never cope with having a child with disabilities." It was about a year later that we realized that our oldest daughter was autistic.

As I look back now, I realize that my daughter is very similar to that little boy I worked with years ago. This was probably a great little guy in many ways, but in my limited time with him, I couldn't get past his extreme behavior to see the child underneath. On the other hand, my daughter also has many extreme behaviors. And yes, they drive me crazy some days. But because she is my child, I am able to work with her and love her despite her behavior. We are the most dedicated teachers our children could ever hope to have. Sometimes we just need to remember that, in order to help us get through those tough days.

One more thing that we should consider if we are Christians is that the ministry of the Holy Spirit is, in part, a ministry of teaching. For Christians, there is an unlimited supply of "adequacy" through the Holy Spirit. Let's not forget to appropriate the power available to us!

When it's just not working

Do I ever think that a parent should not be home schooling a special needs child? Yes, I have run into situations in which I have felt that home schooling wasn't working for a particular family, but these have been rare. Usually, if a mother cannot get past her feelings of inadequacy and get onto more productive issues, home schooling tends to become a joyless, emotionally trying experience—and those are the good days. This tends to reinforce the mother's perception that she is inadequate, and it becomes a vicious cycle. I believe that a good support group can go a long way in helping parents realize their adequacy.

Another reason that I have seen home schooling fail is when parents are not willing to adequately discipline their children because they blame all behavior on the disability. This is not realistic. As I said before, our children are just that—children. Whether "normal" or "disabled" they will be willful, disobedient, and disrespectful at some time or another. When we let our children—any of our children—get away with behavior like this, we do them the gravest disservice possible we can as parents. Even if our children never learn to read and write, if we can take them out in public, and they can be well-behaved, we have accomplished more than many parents with so-called normal children!

CHAPTER 11

Grief

A NOTHER ISSUE THAT we must deal with is our grief. Every parent I talk to, no matter how mild or how severe the disability of their child, has experienced grief upon hearing that their child has a learning difficulty. In order to be effective educators, we must acknowledge this grief and work through it to acceptance. The grief process is well documented, and I know I went through it just like the textbooks say! So have the other mothers in my support group.

Why do we experience grief? Grief is normal with any kind of loss. When we have children with any type of disability, whether it is an attention problem, a reading problem, or something more involved like retardation or autism, this is not the child that we imagined, and we grieve for the "lost" child of our imaginations. Also, it is painful for us as parents to watch our children struggle. So part of the grief is for ourselves, and part is for our children. (I sometimes think that it is most difficult for parents of very mildly learning-disabled children because they do not get the acknowledgement of their grief. These children are totally normal except when it comes to learning, and then it can be a painful process for them and their families. This is often misunderstood by people who haven't "been there," and there can be subtle criticism or lack of compassion.)

The stages of grief are usually the same, but, depending on our own emotional development and the types of disabilities our children have, we may experience some stages more than others. We may also experience some aspects of grief again as our children hit milestones, such as certain birthdays, or when other children begin to have experiences our children cannot be involved in.

I first went through a stage of DENIAL. I couldn't (or wouldn't) accept that my child had any type of real or lasting problem. I figured that if we just worked hard enough, it would eventually go away. When working hard wasn't enough, I began to HOPE we would find the "magic cure." Of course, there isn't one, so when that didn't work, I was ANGRY. As I recounted earlier, I was angry at God, at Alison, and at other people who had children with no problems. I just couldn't get over the fact that all these other people just kept going on with their normal lives while my life had been turned upside down. Next, I began to feel SHAME. I was convinced that other people must think I was less as a parent because I had a child with difficulties. The fact that I did get some unfounded criticism only added to my feelings of worthlessness as a parent. I went through a period of withdrawing from my friends with "normal" children. Fortunately, through the normal passage of time, much prayer, and my wonderful husband, I was able to move out of these stages and into ACCEPTANCE (see below).

There are still times, however, when I grieve for the things my daughter will never do, or for the difficulty she has in social situations, or for myself because working with her is hard and tiring. We may grieve because our children are behind in school, or because they don't have many friends, or because it breaks our hearts to listen to them struggle through a reading lesson. Whatever our feelings, they are valid emotions that we must deal with in order to work effectively with our children. Although grief may come and go at various times, acceptance becomes the key issue for us if we are to effectively educate our children.

CHAPTER 12

Acceptance

(Realistic Expectations for Our Children and Ourselves)

WRAPPED UP TIGHTLY with the grief process is the process of acceptance. I constantly meet people, especially fathers, who feel that if their children just tried harder, all their learning problems would be solved. I also meet people who say they don't want to accept a diagnosis because they feel that means they are giving up on their children. Let me explain why I think that acceptance is so crucial in helping us be effective teachers.

I believe that in order to effectively educate our children we have to have a plan that is both appropriate and realistic. Appropriate planning comes from understanding our children's unique blend of strengths and weaknesses and how they can best learn. We find this out primarily through testing and then educating ourselves about the particular learning problems that our children have. That was what the first section of this book was all about!

But realistic planning can only come from acceptance. I can tell you from personal experience that knowledge and acceptance are two different ball games! When we first realized that our daughter wasn't developing language the way she should, I took her for testing and found out all I could about language delays. I also began to recognize that she had many autistic symptoms, but I kept saying that she had some "autistic-like" behaviors, and I was sure that as soon as we got her language problems taken care of those would go away. In the meantime, I began reading all I could on autism, and, again, I was very knowledgeable. But I kept telling myself that this was not really the problem we were facing. After two years of language/speech therapy that didn't fix the problem, I embarked on my quest for the "magic cure" that I mentioned before. I read all the miracle story books on diet, auditory training, sensory integration, holding therapy, and Lovaas. Nothing was the miracle I wanted, but I still resisted the idea of saying my daughter was autistic. (Don't forget that I went through all of this even though I already had my Master's Degree in Special Education! Knowledge alone does not automatically lead to acceptance).

As I look back, I now realize how this kept me from being realistic in my expectations and my work with my daughter. I was determined to not accept that she might be autistic, so I began to work as hard as I could to make her normal. But the harder I worked and pushed her, the more frustrated and angry I became. My anger became directed towards her, and her behavior worsened instead of improving. When I was finally able to accept the fact that she was autistic, and that no matter how hard I worked or she worked, we would never change that, I was able to relax and create a more realistic program for her that has ultimately been more successful than all the pushing and anger.

Many of you don't have children nearly as severe as my daughter, but in talking with the many people I have worked with in both schools and home schooling, I find this pattern to be the same. Let's say we have a boy who is experiencing some relatively mild difficulties in written language and who has difficulty with attention. Many people would say that those aren't really disabilities, but that's not how it feels to the parents. To them it feels like their child has just as big a disability as my daughter. When the disability is denied by others, it makes it harder for parents to work through and accept the child the way he is instead of the way they wish he were.

Why do we have unrealistic expectations for our children and why is it often so hard for us to accept the learning difficulties that our children have? As I have stated earlier, our society is obsessed with over-achievement. When we do find out that we have children with learning problems, we desperately try everything we can get our hands on to "fix" them so they can be "normal," just as I did. One of the most common questions I am asked after testing a child is, "What do we do, or what can we use to fix this?" Accepting all of our children as God has made them, whether high-achievers, average, learning disabled, or more severely handicapped, will help us to be realistic in our expectations and to set realistic goals for their education.

I think another reason we want to try to make our children "normal" is that we tend to take at least part of our own self worth from our children's achievements. When we have children who don't "measure up" in the eyes of society, it is easy to feel that we don't measure up. This is further compounded when we encounter professionals who view the "norm" as the only desired goal, and that nothing less will do. This only adds to the feelings of worthlessness of the parents who are often already doing the best they can. Because our society is highly literate, and knowledge and literacy are highly valued, it is easy to think that those things are the only measures of our children's (and by extension, our) worth. Of course, some weaknesses can be strengthened or even remediated with the proper therapy, and, if that is the case, then those goals are realistic; but many learning difficulties are not "fixable." That doesn't mean that we are any less because we can't do the impossible!

I believe that there are two things we need to do when we start feeling that our children's difficulties are a reflection on us. First, we need to educate ourselves thoroughly about the particular learning problem our child faces. (I know I keep saying this, but I can't stress enough the importance of accurate knowledge to the success of our schooling efforts.) We need to know what the realistic expectations for this child are. What parts of his learning problems are possibly open for remediation, and what parts do we need to just accept and work with the best we can to bring him to his highest potential.

Of course, it may be easier to agree with that in our heads than in our hearts. We may have friends or even family members who feel we are just not working hard enough, or we are too soft on little Johnny, or we don't discipline enough or in the right way, or... I could go on and on. You know the comments or the feelings you get from other people. When my daughter was younger and would throw one of her screaming tantrums in a store, I would get the "bad mother" looks from people too. (In my less charitable moments I have thought of having a T-shirt printed that says, "I'm Autistic. What's Your Problem?" but I know that wouldn't be very nice. Still, there are those days....)

Whether it is a grandparent who just can't accept that Susie wouldn't have a reading problem if she just weren't so lazy, or people in the grocery store who have gotten my little "crash course" in autism, the idea is the same—when we stop feeling guilty or responsible for our children's difficulties, we can deal openly and confidently with other people. And I think our positive, accepting attitudes carry over to other people and, most importantly, to our children.

Second, we need to focus on our children's strengths and abilities. It is so easy to become consumed with our children's difficulties that we can forget about the things they can do. Seeing more than just our children's weaknesses can help us be realistic in a positive way. Again, though, we have to be careful not to take the "norm" as our only measure. Some strengths are relative to the child but still may not reach "normal." That is OK. If it is a relative strength, we need to recognize it and build on it just the same. And remembering to build on strengths can make our goals and our teaching much more realistic.

For example, we hear so much about how phonics is the only "good" way to teach reading. However, if I had a child with an auditory processing difficulty who is not learning to read using phonics but has great visual skills, I would be silly not to use those visual skills to begin teaching reading by sight while working on phonics as a side issue in an effort to build auditory skills. Yet, so many times we think that our children must learn the way "normal" children do, or we have failed. Looking realistically at our children's strengths can help us use more appropriate teaching methods for those children and can keep us reasonably sane in the process! We'll look at using strengths again when we begin discussing the process of planning your program.

CHAPTER 13

Anger

I HAVE ALREADY mentioned anger as part of grief, but sometimes anger can take on a "life of its own," apart from its place in the grieving process. This is also something that needs to be honestly addressed in order to effectively teach our children.

Anger can come from many of the different frustrations we encounter in teaching a special needs child. Sometimes we may be angry at God for the difficulties our child has. That anger can be self-destructive, as it often turns into bitterness and begins to turn itself on the child as well. Sometimes we may be angry at behavior issues that persist despite the fact that we have "done all the right things." Sometimes we are angry at our child because we have explained that concept or rule or math problem four times already and they still don't get it or remember it. Sometimes we are angry that other people have children who are doing so much better than our children, and that no one seems to have a clue that what we do every day is hard.

These are all legitimate reasons why we may experience anger. The key is to not feel guilty when it happens but to recognize that it is part and parcel of having and teaching a child with learning problems. The fact is that we are going to feel angry about our situation or at our children from time to time. What we have to work through is to not let anger consume us, but rather to recognize it and deal with it appropriately.

I used to think that it was wrong to get angry. I thought that, as a Christian, I should never get angry (or at least I shouldn't let it show)! When I was teaching junior high school, however, I had a very wise principal who taught me that anger is not bad in and of itself, but it can be bad or good depending on how we react to it and how we channel it.

This can be especially true of teaching our special needs children. If I get angry at my circumstances and my child's learning problems, I can let that anger fester and take it out on my child, my husband, and my dog; or I can channel that anger into positive action that gives me the drive to keep on working and pushing forward even when the progress is slow or seems nonexistent.

Another issue that often comes up when discussing anger is that sometimes it is our children who are angry! This most often occurs when we have a child who is very bright, but has some kind of specific learning disability. One of the reasons that I am usually an advocate of explaining a child's disability to him is that children who are struggling often blame themselves for their learning problems. Because they are bright they feel that they should be able to read or write better and they often become angry at themselves or think there is something wrong with them. With children like this, being up-front with them about their learning difficulties is an important part of helping them learn to cope with real life issues and difficulties.

Sometimes our children are also angry at God for making them "different." This most often occurs at adolescence, when being different is the worst thing in the world! When this happens, we need to acknowledge our children's anger and let them know that it is OK to express that anger to God. We need to also communicate the truth that God made them for a purpose—to glorify Him and bring His love to their world, and we need to encourage them to find ways of living out God's purpose for their lives.

CHAPTER 14

Discouragement Over Progress

DISCOURAGEMENT SHOULD BE labeled "public enemy number one" for home schooling moms! Again we need to have a realistic view of our children's abilities and disabilities and what we can realistically do as teachers. We are not miracle workers. God may give miracles to some, but to be perfectly honest here, I'm tired of the miracle cure books. This happens to truly a small percentage of the people who have special needs children. The vast majority of us are just plodding along from day to day, trying to teach our children to the best of our abilities, sometimes with limited cooperation from the children themselves, while also attempting to put dinner on the table and maintain good relationships with our husbands.

How can you effectively deal with discouragement? One thing you may need to do is to change your perspective. If your child didn't progress as much as you wanted him to, did he progress at all? Keep in mind that small progress is still progress and needs to be counted and celebrated, not looked at as "not enough."

We also need to look for other areas that your child may have grown in that didn't show up as academic progress. For example, did he grow in frustration tolerance, cooperative attitude, or organizational skills? These areas may not show up on any testing but they are just as important.

Support can be another important ingredient to battling discouragement. There is something reassuring about hearing that other home school parents are struggling with the same issues and feelings that we are struggling with.

Another thing that we need to consider when we don't see progress with our children is whether or not we are pushing them through tough areas or backing down too easily and not setting our standards high enough. Although it is difficult for some of us, there are areas and times when we must make our children do things that are tough for them in order for progress to occur. Sometimes an outside therapist can be helpful with this (so that she can be the "bad guy").

Humor is also an antidote to discouragement. I find that I most often get discouraged when I am too serious about life. Sometimes I just need to lighten up a bit and laugh along with my child and enjoy her instead of worrying and over-analyzing every difficulty she has or could have in the future! Let's face it; if we back up a little and look at our children a little more objectively, some of the things they do and say are funny. Humor also has the potential for diffusing tense situations. When I find myself getting too uptight over behavior or discouraged over lack of progress, I find that injecting some laughter into the day can relax everyone. And it's amazing how much more progress is made and how much better everyone's attitudes are on those days!

I have also found it important to keep an eternal perspective when I find myself getting discouraged. I so often need to take off my "disability blinders" and step back so that I can see the whole picture. When I remember that our lives here on earth are microscopic compared with the time we will spend in heaven, I realize that all of Alison's difficulties and all of our struggles will be over in an instant. One of the things I am looking forward to in heaven is having a conversation with my daughter and hearing her voice! When I think of that, it helps me put all that I do with her in perspective. How much more important is her soul and the spiritual development of our whole family than whether or not "x" amount of progress was made in our reading program.

CHAPTER 15

No Time for Me!

ALTHOUGH THIS IS not necessarily an emotional issue unique to home schoolers of special needs children, I think we sometimes have more difficulty making time for ourselves than other home schooling moms. It is a tired saying, but true, that if mom doesn't take care of herself, she can't take care of anyone else. And because we have to pour so much of our energy into our special needs children, we may burn out faster and brighter if we don't give ourselves the rest and refreshment we need.

Years ago, I heard Bill Hybels speak about our three tanks that need to stay filled if we are to remain emotionally healthy. He stated that many people understand that they need to replenish themselves physically and spiritually, but many of us forget to make sure we replenish ourselves emotionally. He then added that if we have any ongoing emotional drains, such as having a disabled child, we need to be extra sensitive to taking time away to refresh ourselves. I'll never forget how grateful I was to hear a pastor make a statement like that. It felt so good to hear that someone seemed to understand that I had special needs too, not just my child! But I was even more grateful when the group of people I was with practically jumped on me after the conference session wanting to know it was true that I was already emotionally drained just from having Alison. When I told them that I often feel emotionally drained, they all said they had never thought about that before, and they would be sure to pray specifically for my emotional health!

That experience taught me something important. The people around us may be wonderful people, but they have no way of knowing our needs unless we clue them in. And I thought it was so obvious! But in conversing with my friends that night, I realized that my needs were not that obvious. In fact, the better we are at coping and carrying on, the less people will perceive us as having special needs. Now that doesn't mean that we want to be basket cases all the time just so people will know we have needs—our friends would get tired of that very quickly. But it does mean that we should not be afraid to articulate our need to get out of the house and away from our children sometimes, because it is the only way people will really know.

I have found this to be true even of my husband. I used to get very upset because he didn't know when I was struggling or feeling discouraged over Alison's behavior or lack of progress that day. But it finally hit me that I had no idea what went on with him all day either. I just expected that because he came home to the same house that I had been in all day, he automatically saw (or sensed) what had gone on during the day. Of course, as soon as I realized how I had been thinking, I could see that it was ridiculous! How could he know what I was feeling or thinking or even what had happened ten minutes before he walked in the door, much less at 9 a.m. As soon as I realized that unless I told him that I had had a bad day and would be in the bathtub for one hour ("don't call me unless the house is on fire!"), he would never know. It was amazing that as soon as I started telling him honestly, and, I might add here, without anger, how I felt and what I needed, I started feeling a lot less needy. And he started picking up on some of the more subtle signals of my stress!

If you have difficulty telling other people that you need a break, consider this: stress makes you a less effective teacher of your child. I read of a recent study of a home-based program for severely handicapped children that linked low stress levels of the parents with the children who had the highest rate of progress in the program. So even if you have trouble seeking relief for yourself, remember that you are benefiting your children by doing what you need to do to regroup emotionally.

One reason it is easy to get trapped at home is because we are reluctant to leave our children who have behavior problems with sitters. Although we may be able to get out alone sometimes when our husbands watch the children, this doesn't give us the opportunity to spend time alone with our husbands which is equally important. If we do not have other family members who can learn to manage our children, we should consider checking at our local universities for students working on their special education credentials. They may be more than willing to learn how to manage our children for one afternoon a week because they often need to observe children and write case studies for school anyway! I have to admit that I have had a lot of help with my children. One thing I have found over the years is that every time I have needed help, God has faithfully provided. So if you are feeling stuck on where to get some help, I advise you to go straight to God and ask Him to provide. And then, be willing to use the people He sends your way!

CHAPTER 16

Our Other Children

The Balancing Act

ANOTHER ISSUE THAT is often a concern to the people I work with is worry over their other children. Will working with a special needs learner allow them enough time for their other children? On the other hand, will they be able to give the special learner the time he needs while still doing all the things they want to do with their other children? I have truly seen almost as many solutions to this difficulty as the number of people I work with. This is because each family is unique. However, I will discuss some of the ideas I've seen (and used myself), and you can adapt them for your situation.

One of the most common solutions is to put the other children in school and only home school the special learner. I have worked with many families who have done this. There are pros and cons to this approach. An obvious pro is that you have uninterrupted one-on-one time with your special learner.

However, sometimes the child who stays home feels that it is a punishment for having learning problems, and sometimes the children going off to school feel that they are being punished because the other child "gets" to stay home. I do know of families in which the dynamics were such that the younger children were so far ahead of the children with the learning problems that it caused added frustration and stress to the entire family. In those cases, having the other children go to school has seemed to lessen the stress and has worked well.

I tried this for one year, and it really didn't work for me. I put my younger child in preschool one year to try and work more intensively with my daughter who has autism. Not only was I driving around a lot, but Laura, who went to school, complained that she wanted to stay home, and Alison, who came home with me, always tried to follow Laura into the classroom and cried when we left! I have definitely had more success with having everyone at home.

A variation on this idea is to do some kind of co-oping. I've done several different types of co-ops over the years. Most have focused, in one form or another, on history and science one day a week with all other work being done at home. Some years we had multiple children with learning issues and were able to accommodate and support each other. Other years, Alison was the only special needs student. Those co-op experiences were focused more on the needs of my other children. One year, my mother-in-law came and was an "aide" in the Kindergarten-First Grade program so that Alison could hang out in there while I taught Jr. High History (a welcome change for me!).

Another idea is to be less of a perfectionist with the children who can do more on their own. We may love doing projects and want to be involved in all of our more capable child's stuff, but maybe we just need to back off and let them do more on their own while we spend the one-on-one time with our special learners. I have often taken a "bare bones" approach with my more capable children over the years. When Laura was younger, I gave her certain tasks that she had to accomplish, and for most everything else we used a literature approach in which we read and discussed topics. As she got older, she designed many of her own courses (especially in high school) based on her interests, and I worked with her in areas that were more difficult such as Algebra. My son needed more one-on-one help when he was younger learning to read—so at that point, actually Alison had to have less of my time. As Logan became more capable, we again did a lot of reading together and discussion, but he has a high need for structure, so for many of his subjects we have gone to computer based learning. We have used both Switched-On-Schoolhouse (www.aop.com) and Time 4 Learning (www.time4learning.com) and those have been a good fit for his learning style.

Emotional Issues

What about issues that come up between siblings as a result of learning problems? A potentially painful problem, especially for the bright learning-disabled child, is having a younger sibling pass an older one academically. As I mentioned before, this has been one reason that some of the families I work with have put their younger children in school. But how do we deal with the emotions of the older children regardless of where the younger children are during school time? This is another reason that I am very much in favor of children knowing as much as they can understand about their own disabilities. Children, especially those with average to above average intelligence who have specific learning disabilities, need to know the cause of their own learning difficulties. As I mentioned before, when we are not up-front with these children, they come up with much worse explanations than the truth. Usually, they decide that they are stupid or somehow to blame for their learning problems.

Sometimes, I have heard the objection that if we tell a bright child that he has a disability, he will use it as an excuse to not do his best work. Although it is normal for children to try to use excuses to get out of anything they don't like, I believe that thinking they are stupid is worse than trying to get out of work! It is, for the most part, our responsibility to set clear and reasonable expectations for our children, to make it clear that what we expect is appropriate for them, and then to not allow them to use excuses.

On the other hand, it may be our more capable children who are distraught because we give the special learner more of our individual time and attention. If that is the case, we may need to spend less one-on-one time with our special needs learners and add some small amounts of one-on-one time for our other children. Some things can also be done together, such as listening to oral reading, that are non-competitive, but that every child can get something out of at their own level.

Character Development

I truly believe that growing up in a household with a special needs child is a unique opportunity for our other children. God has not made a mistake with our families. Acceptance, which we discussed earlier, when practiced by us is transferred to our children. I was struck by a comment my daughter Laura made one day when I was expecting our third child. She asked if I thought the baby might be blind or deaf or have any kind of handicap. I said I didn't know and asked why she was wondering that. She replied that she had just been thinking that if the baby were blind, she would have to learn Braille, just as she was learning to sign because of Alison. "Anyway," she added, "in heaven Alison will be able to talk just like us, so if this baby is blind or something, it will go away when we get to heaven!"

As I reflected on that conversation, it struck me that Laura didn't think of a handicap as necessarily a bad thing, just something that might happen, and she wanted to be prepared! When our children see us love and accept someone who is "different," those differences don't matter as much, and I think their character will be developed and refined in wonderful ways.

CHAPTER 17

The Socialization Issue

EVERY HOME SCHOOLING family eventually gets asked about socialization, but if we are home schooling special needs children, this issue seems to become an even greater concern. After all, aren't social skills a big problem for most of our kids? How will they ever learn social behavior without peer modeling? Well, let's look a little more closely at the social needs of special children.

A special needs child has the same social needs that every other child has. This may seem obvious, but it is important to keep in mind, especially if we have children who withdraw from social situations. Every child needs to learn how to interact successfully with other people (of all ages) and how to behave in a manner that is deemed appropriate and acceptable to each situation. These are the two basic social needs of every child. The degree to which children learn how to successfully interact and behave will determine the depth of the relationships that they can develop.

In special needs children, these skills—like most of their skills—are slower to develop and many of the social skills that other children pick up environmentally need to be directly taught. It is important to keep in mind that social development is tied to cognitive development in many ways. Children who interact and behave in socially acceptable ways do so because they have learned how to judge what is and is not socially acceptable. This ability is closely linked to cognitive development. For example, younger children (below age eight) use a law and order reasoning to determine what is right and wrong socially. Things they will get in trouble for are wrong, things that they are praised for are right. As children gain more cognitive reasoning ability, they move into more sophisticated ways of determining appropriateness. For example, they learn to view things from another's perspective, they learn concepts of kindness and fairness, they learn to read facial expressions and body language, and they learn to change their behavior in response to other people's reactions. All of these skills require cognitive abilities beyond the simple right and wrong stage. However, most special needs children are either significantly behind their peers in cognitive development or they have difficulties with things such as impulse control or language that make it more difficult for them to interact appropriately.

Teaching social skills to special needs children is very much like teaching social skills to toddlers—it often seems as if you are not getting anywhere! Perseverance is definitely a key! Aside from that, there are three key ingredients to teaching social skills to special needs children: direct instruction, practice, and teaching self-monitoring skills.

It is my belief that these skills are best taught in the family setting before (and while) branching out into other social settings. Gregg Harris in his book, *The Christian Home School,* describes age-segregated socialization as children pooling their collective inexperience! When you add special needs to that, children in age-segregated, disability-segregated classrooms are often pooling not only their inexperience, but often their inappropriate behaviors as well! On the other hand, by having our children within the family unit, they are receiving better modeling of appropriate behaviors as well as the opportunity for direct instruction of and practice of appropriate behaviors in a supportive, loving atmosphere where rejection and ridicule are not part of the daily experience.

Let's take a brief look at each of the key ingredients for teaching social skills.

Direct Instruction: For most children with learning problems, having appropriate social skills modeled for them (while important) is not nearly enough. For most of these children, skills must be taught directly and in the most concrete terms possible. For example, don't worry about teaching concepts such as fairness if your child is not cognitively able to understand that concept. Instead, teach the behavior that you want as a rule of conduct. For example, special needs children often have difficulty responding when someone greets them. Discussing issues such as politeness or simply modeling this behavior won't get you too far. Teaching a child that it is a rule that when someone says "Hi" then the child says "Hi" is much more effective.

Practice: Once you teach a social rule, your child must be able to practice it. However, instead of throwing him into a group of children for socialization, practice of social skills is much more effective in small, age-integrated groups with parent support. Have people into your home where you can remind your child of proper social behavior, and if necessary, guide him through the types of social skills you have been teaching (saying hi, taking turns, sharing, etc.). When skills like this are practiced under your supervision with other understanding parents and children, much more real socialization is taking place than when children with difficulties are thrown into large groups of people who are not prepared to understand their needs. Learning to get along and respond correctly to a wide range of people is more socializing in the long run and occurs naturally as you practice hospitality in your home.

Self-Monitoring: Although the family and the home are the ideal settings for teaching and practicing social skills, we all must venture out into the wider world, and our children need to be taught how to self-monitor their behavior when they are away from us. For some very severely disabled children, self-monitoring may not be possible; but for older and less disabled children this is the most crucial step in the process of socialization.

Remember, socialization can be boiled down to two basic parts: successful interactions and appropriate behavior. When we teach a child the correct way to respond when addressed (by saying hi) and give him opportunities to practice greeting people, we must then teach him to evaluate his own behavior after the social exchange has taken place (self-monitoring).

Teaching self-monitoring involves helping children learn how to review proper behavior before going into a social situation and then evaluate themselves afterwards. This takes a lot of help and scripting at first, but with practice it can become a very effective way of helping children with learning problems participate successfully in social situations without help. I'll continue with the example of greeting someone to show how self-monitoring might look. After teaching the child to look someone in the eye and say hi, you would then teach him to remind himself of what he needs to do before entering a social situation. At first you would prompt him by asking, "What will you do when someone says hi?" and having him explain what he will do. After the social time is over, ask him to evaluate how he did by saying, "When someone said hi, what did you do?" You can then discuss whether or not he was able to practice what he had learned and praise any progress. This takes a lot of work and a lot of time, but it is well worth the effort.

Our children may always struggle in social settings more than other children. They may need constant reminding and self-monitoring in order to have successful interactions, and it may never be easy or comfortable for them. Sometimes it is easy to feel embarrassed or sad over the social difficulties that our children experience, but our children don't have to have perfect social skills to be the people God intended for them to be. Don't forget to look for the social strengths in your child. For example, Alison has learned recently to ask each person who comes into our home if they would like a cup of coffee. This is not only quite an accomplishment for her, but it is charming and sweet. We must never think these types of accomplishments are less because of other problems. I also doubt that she would have developed this skill if she had been isolated from our family for most of each day becoming socialized into the disabled world of special education. Think about it.

RESOURCES FOR SOCIAL SKILLS

Navigating the Social World, Jeanette McAfee, M.D.
A curriculum for individuals with Asperger's Syndrome, High Functioning Autism, and Related Disorders. This important new book offers a definitive program with forms, exercises, and guides for the student. It also presents significant educational guidance and supportive ideas for parents. (www.avcsbooks.com)

LinguiSystems (www.linguisystems.com)
They carry many social skills and social language books. I've never been disappointed with any of their products.

CHAPTER 18

Behavior Problems

F INALLY, WE MUST address the behavior difficulties that most of our children demonstrate. Behavior problems can be roadblocks to effective home schooling for two reasons. First of all, our children's difficult behavior can sometimes feel like the "last straw." It's bad enough that we have to re-teach concepts and facts over and over, but to have to deal with some of our children's behavior can be really hard emotionally. Here again, I believe that knowledge is power. Knowing that some of the difficult behaviors our children exhibit is a "normal" part of their disabilities can make dealing with them somewhat easier.

Second, behavior is a crucial aspect in creating an effective home school program because, if our children cannot behave, they cannot learn. Even if we effectively deal with all of the other issues we have discussed, our home school program will ultimately be unsuccessful unless we teach our children to behave in a reasonable manner. It is sometimes too easy to pity our children and not demand enough of them when it comes to behavior. As I stated before, our children must still learn obedience, respect, and self-control. It is tempting to attribute all of our children's poor behavior to their learning difficulties, but this is not realistic. Our children are still children, disabled or not, and some of their behavior will be just a result of their childishness.

Helen Keller was an excellent example of a disabled child who was pitied and never required to behave. When her teacher, Anne Sullivan, came to work with her, she could make no progress in teaching Helen because of the girl's terrible behavior. Only after Miss Sullivan established discipline and expectations for Helen's behavior could they begin to make progress in learning.

It is, of course, important to strike a balance here between no expectations and unrealistic expectations. Some of our children will have behavior difficulties that will not go away, no matter how reasonable and consistent our behavior training and expectations are. But even if our children have behaviors that are extreme and persistent, you must always demand basic obedience. My own daughter, for example, was extremely resistant to structured learning tasks and used to throw screaming temper tantrums when she had to do something that was difficult (or not of her choosing). It would have been much easier to back down whenever she did this because it is hard to deal with. However, my expectations were reasonable, so I demanded that she obey me and come to the task. The persistence has paid off in both her behavior and in her ability to work through difficult material. However, this doesn't mean her behavior is perfect. Many of the specific behaviors our children have are wrapped up in their different disabilities and may never disappear completely, but we must deal with them as best we can while still demanding obedience and the best behavior possible from the child.

Notice that I said deal with, not solve. We set ourselves up for a lot of discouragement and self-recrimination when we think that we should be able to solve all of our children's difficulties. Instead, it is more realistic to look at ways to manage our children's behavior and to teach them as best we can to be self-controlled. Our children will be happier, more productive people, in the long run, for our efforts.

Let's now look specifically at some of the typical behavior problems that special needs children demonstrate and some methods for dealing with these behavior difficulties.

When looking at behavior, it is important to realize that many of our children exhibit behaviors which might be immature for their ages, but developmentally appropriate. For example, it is "normal" for two-year-olds to have tantrums as part of their developmental process. So if an older child who is developing slowly suddenly begins throwing tantrums we wouldn't necessarily panic, but would instead, work through this behavior as with a younger child.

Also, some children have inappropriate or bizarre behaviors, but these are usually confined to the more severe disabilities and don't necessarily interfere directly with learning; so I won't be addressing them specifically. Examples of these types of behaviors include eating inedible objects, removing clothes at inappropriate times/places, and compulsive or ritualistic types of behaviors. Behavior modification techniques seem to be the most effective tools for managing these behaviors (this will be discussed below), but they often provide only management, not elimination of the problem behaviors. In some cases, medication may also be helpful in controlling bizarre behaviors.

Other than that, I see behavior difficulties falling into three main types: Attention Difficulties (distractibility, impulsiveness, hyperactivity, or perseveration), Resistant Behaviors (tantrums, screaming, or whining due to low frustration tolerance), and Passive Behaviors (withdrawal, passive resistance [the "I don't know" / "I can't" syndrome] and lack of motivation).

Why do these behaviors occur? There are countless factors that can contribute to behavior difficulties, but some of the reasons include low tolerance for frustration, poor self-image due to past failures, and over-reaction to environmental noise or commotion. Some are simply due to the neurological makeup of our children such as attention difficulties and hyperactive behaviors. Poor language skills can also add to the behavior difficulties our children may already have. Many children misinterpret instructions because of poor processing or vocabulary and may overreact to misunderstood demands. A child with poor word-retrieval skills may not be able to find the words to make a verbal protest and so sulks or has a temper tantrum instead. Children with behavior difficulties often key off of the level of stress surrounding them, so doing as much as possible to reduce our own stress and the stress levels in our homes can also be somewhat helpful. But whatever the reason, we must find appropriate ways of dealing with and managing the difficult behaviors our children exhibit.

What's Normal?

When choosing how to deal with certain behaviors, we often need to be able to tell whether the behavior is normal, childish behavior, which may need to be punished, or behavior caused by frustration or fear of failure. Sometimes it is very difficult. I know, for me, it is often a process of trial and error. For example, when my daughter becomes resistant, I try to look objectively at what we are doing. Is this something we've done before with success? If so, I tend to be more inclined to think that her resistance is childish, and I deal with it as a discipline issue. Is this a new task or something we haven't done in a while? Then I tend to think it may be more frustration related, and I back off or restructure the task. The thing to remember is that we often do make mistakes. I have probably disciplined her for just being frustrated, and I have probably backed off at times when I should have pushed. Just as our children are not perfect learners, we are not perfect teachers. Ask God for wisdom, and then go with what seems most appropriate.

A related issue that we need to acknowledge is that sometimes we can take our children's behavior too personally—as if they are doing this to us instead of just being childish or frustrated. I know that nothing can get me more upset than my daughter's tantrums, especially if I don't feel her resistance is from frustration. But we do need to remember that the learning process is often very painful for our children. We may find ways that they enjoy learning more, we may tap into their interests and we may plan great hands-on activities; but the bottom line is that no matter what we do, some things will still be difficult, some things will still be painful, and sometimes our children are just children—foolish and disobedient. On one very bad day, I sent everyone back to bed (including me). Don't despair on days like that. Take it as an opportunity to build character and discipline—and maybe a way to get a nap as well!

Methods for Dealing with Difficult Behavior

Behavior Modification

Behavior modification refers to the concept that if we *reward* the behavior we want, it will increase; and if we *punish or ignore* the behavior we don't want, it will decrease. It is a very simple and quite effective concept when used correctly. I have heard objections to using behavior modification which I'd like to address briefly. Some people feel uncomfortable with the concept of rewards reasoning that we are paying or bribing children to do what they should be doing in the first place. Although this is somewhat true, I feel that we all work on some kind of a reward system, whether we recognize it or not. We go to work for a paycheck; but even when we do volunteer work, we get "paid" through recognition or praise and if we don't we feel slighted! Many of our children, especially those who are passive or resistant learners, respond to rewards because they see little value in the learning task itself.

Another complaint I hear about behavior modification techniques is that there is no "heart"; that working with children in this way is cold and rigid. When we read some of the ideas for punishing extreme behaviors or some of the techniques for making children stay at task, it is easy to think that everything about behavior modification is cold and rigid. However, any of us working with children who demonstrate extreme behaviors know that sometimes we need to be tough in order to get anywhere. Also, these techniques are very clinical sounding when we read them, but we bring our own personalities (and love) into them when we use them; and the way we implement these ideas does not have to be cold or rigid. I often take behavior modification-type ideas that sound very rigid and modify them to fit my own personality and situation.

And finally, many people are concerned because the concept of behavior modification addresses only the behavior and not the motivation behind it. They argue that using these techniques will not teach our children the idea of being good out of moral character and a desire to please God. That is quite true. These techniques are only useful to teach or control behavior, not character. Character is something that we, as parents, have to model for our children, no matter what techniques we use for behavior and discipline.

How can we use this technique effectively with our children? First of all, we need to realize that using rewards, punishment, or ignoring is no substitute for modeling and teaching character. Our example will always be the most important teaching tool we can use, but the behavior modification techniques can be good tools to help us mold our children's behavior when they are first learning.

Rewards

Reward systems work best if they are simple, immediate, meaningful to the child, consistent, and faded out over time. A sticker chart is a good example of a simple reward system. We list out the things that we want to see, and give a sticker or star, etc., each time that behavior is completed. A chart is also easy to modify as needed. For example, one of my daughters would do each task on her chart, but she would complain her way through it! After establishing what needed to be done, I went back through her chart and added the word "cheerfully" to each item. Now she no longer got a star for emptying the dishwasher, but only for emptying the dishwasher cheerfully!

Reward systems that are immediate are also more effective. Stickers are a good example of an immediate reward. Food is another example. For most children, if the reward is too far in the future, they lose sight of their goals and have difficulty maintaining the required behaviors. One way around this is to give stickers or stars that can be redeemed for bigger rewards after so many have been earned. Another way to help children work toward longer-range goals is to have a picture of the goal to help them visualize amounts of time. One of the rewards I used with Alison when she was young was to be able to watch a Disney video after she completed her school work. However, she had difficulty associating her work with the reward, so I would sometimes put the movie box next to where we were working so that she could see what she was working for. (Sometimes this was too distracting; I would have to gauge her emotional "mood" before I decided if this was appropriate on that day.)

Reward systems must also be meaningful to the child in order to be effective. This is probably one of the most overlooked aspects of reward systems. If stickers are not meaningful to our children, using a sticker chart will not increase the behavior we want no matter how persistent we are. For my daughter, touch ("high-fives," hugs, sitting on my lap) and verbal praise are things that are meaningful to her, so those are usually her immediate rewards. I've worked with other children who looked down their noses at stickers but would work for free time or reduced homework. We have to find what will motivate each child and use that.

Rewards must also be consistent, which means that once we establish a system (using a chart or checklist for example) we have to use it consistently for a long enough period of time to see results. I know from personal experience that it is easier to establish these systems than to follow through with them! I don't know why this is, except that it does take some time and energy to remember to check the chart, give the sticker, etc., and it is not the kind of thing that we may be used to doing. But unless we use any system with some consistency, it won't have a chance to work.

On the other hand, the strange thing about reward systems is that they lose their effectiveness over time, so they need to be faded out. This means that after we have used a system consistently for awhile and have begun to see results, we need to start skipping days of giving the rewards, while still requiring the behavior (this actually occurs rather naturally; we don't make an issue out of skipping the reward). After awhile, the chart is simply "forgotten," but the desired behaviors should remain!

Punishment

Behavior modification has two different ways of dealing with undesirable behavior—punishing or ignoring. Punishment is something that we, as parents, are all familiar with! This is sometimes the easier method for us to use but is actually not always the most effective. One way to incorporate punishment in a more effective way is to link it to the reward system. For example, if we are giving stars for desired behavior, we can also take away stars for undesirable behaviors! This works best if the stars are being accumulated for larger rewards, but some young children are devastated at simply having the stickers removed from the chart. The most common kinds of punishment, such as spankings or time-outs, are more effective for defiant or out-of-control behavior and really should not be over used.

Another way to make the use of punishment more effective is to make the "punishment fit the crime." This usually involves having specific consequences set up ahead of time for certain misbehavior. For example, we may set up a consequence that states, "If you are mean to your brother, you will have to do his chores for that day."

Ignoring

Ignoring is a very powerful tool that is often neglected in favor of punishment but can be extremely effective for dealing with misbehavior that is an effort to gain our attention. When we ignore behaviors, such as whining or tantrums, we take away the motivation for much of this behavior. Now this isn't always easy to do, especially because when we first ignore a behavior it tends to get worse. But perseverance (and maybe ear plugs!) will pay off with most children. Time-out can be a form of ignoring, if it is used as a way of helping the child get control of himself apart from everyone else, and not as a punishment. Another technique called "The Broken Record" is a form of ignoring. In this technique, we state what we want them to do, and if they protest or whine or throw a tantrum, we ignore what they say or do and just keep repeating the directions.

One very important thing to remember about any type of behavior management is that it never works in real life the way it works in the books! For many children with extreme behaviors, these techniques will not alleviate the behavior as much as offer some control and improvement some of the time.

Breaks

This may seem like a silly "technique" since it is so common-sense, but I often find (and I know it's easy to have this tendency myself) that parents are sometimes reluctant to give breaks when children are being inattentive or frustrated, thinking that they are letting their children "win" and get out of work. While it is true that it is not good to let our children quit when things are difficult or when their attention wanders, stopping for a short stretch or snack break and then returning to the task and finishing it is a helpful technique. It sends two important messages to our children. First, we let them know that we understand their difficulties, while at the same time teaching them to persevere through a task despite those difficulties.

Choices

This is one way to give a resistant learner some control. We might say, "We are going to do reading, math, and computer today. Which one would you like to do first?" In this way we've established our expectations for the day, but allowed some choice on the part of the children, too.

Contracts

A contract is a form of behavior management much like a reward system, but it is a little more sophisticated for use with older children. The idea behind a contract is that it is negotiated between the parent and the child, giving the child some of the responsibility for deciding on appropriate behaviors, rewards, and consequences. When children have a hand in setting up contracts for behavior, they tend to be more apt to try to stick to them (and I have found that they often come up with harsher consequences than I would have!). An example of a contract might be something like this:

> I, John Student, agree to do my math assignment without arguing or slamming my math book on the table. If my assignment is difficult, I agree to ask for help in a respectful manner. For every argument or temper outburst, I agree to do an extra chore after I complete my school work. For every day that I demonstrate self-control, I will earn thirty minutes of Nintendo-playing time.

> I, Jane Parent, agree to explain John's assignment to him and to answer questions when they are asked respectfully. I agree not to lecture when he has an outburst, but to just assign an extra chore. I will keep track of, and reward, his Nintendo time at the end of the week.

Contracts such as this can help take some of the emotional reaction out of dealing with ongoing, difficult behavior because the unacceptable behavior, consequences, acceptable behavior, and rewards are all spelled out clearly ahead of time. There are many good examples of behavior contracts on the internet. Type "behavior contract" into Google and you'll be able to see lots of examples.

Medication

When used responsibly, medication can sometimes help control more extreme attention, hyperactive, or bizarre behaviors so that learning can take place. As I have stated, however, medication is never a cure-all. It can, in some cases, be a part of the puzzle which allows us to make headway in teaching self-control and academics, where it was impossible before.

Pushing and Pulling Back

Sometimes behavior problems begin because what we are doing is truly too hard. If a particular subject is the focus of most of the difficulties we are experiencing, we should try backing off just a notch to review previous material and then reintroduce the difficult material. If that doesn't work, we should consider setting aside what we are doing for a month and then coming back to it.

On the other hand, it is sometimes important to push through difficult behavior. For example, many children will act like any new material is too hard, simply because it is new. If we pick up a pattern like this, it is important that we not back off but instead insist on effort, and support them through the introduction of the new material.

"One More Rule"

If a child has been working satisfactorily on something, but suddenly turns resistant or withdraws, he may have reached the saturation point. But we shouldn't end our teaching on a resistance wins note. Instead, we should say, "We have just one more to do and then we're finished for right now. You're doing a good job; let's finish the last one!"

Relaxation and Coping Skills

Often children demonstrate resistant or passive behaviors because of their own emotional reaction to work or situations that they perceive as impossible. For these children, it is important to directly teach coping skills and relaxation skills. One book that I have found helpful for teaching relaxation is *Aromatherapy and Massage for People with Learning Difficulties.* The book *The Out-of-Sync Child* also offers many good ideas for calming activities. Other ideas for helping children learn to relax and cope with difficulties are to teach deep breathing for calming and relaxation and to stop to pray. We need to demonstrate to our children that when things get difficult, we can stop, regroup, bring our difficulties to the Lord, and then go on. One of the most joyous experiences I had recently was when my daughter came up to me when she was having difficulty with her behavior and signed that she wanted Jesus to help her! We stopped right then and I prayed with her, and we were both able to regroup and calm down.

Praise

Although praise could be viewed as a reward, it can be such a powerful tool for working with passive or withdrawn children that it deserves special attention. Working with passive learners requires a lot of discernment because it is easy to feel too sorry for these children! If we have children who withdraw and tend to cry easily over work that is "just too hard," focusing on the things they have done right can help them cope with having to work through difficult material. But we must be careful to be sincere. Passive learners are usually very emotionally sensitive and will spot phony praise a mile away.

Setting Standards

Setting standards and not backing down even if the tears come can be hard for us moms, but it is so important. We don't do our children any favors by giving in to their tears, as long as our standards are reasonable.

Self-Talk—Stop, Relax, Think, Choose

This technique goes by many names, but the idea is to teach children who get over stimulated or overwhelmed with emotion to stop themselves from throwing tantrums or crying, to relax and think about what they need to do, and then to choose to calm down instead of becoming out of control. At first, you take the child step by step through this process while emphasizing the key words Stop, Relax, Think, Choose. The idea is that, eventually, you should be able to help him by just saying the key words, then by just saying STOP, and finally, he should be able to talk himself through the whole calming process. I use this strategy with both of my daughters who tend to over-react emotionally, and it has been quite helpful. Actually, this technique has been helpful to me, too! The idea of stopping before I over-react to their overreacting has been good, although I need to do it more consistently (we're all learning aren't we!).

Timers

Using timers can be an effective method for dealing with a variety of behaviors. Timers can be useful to help capable but dawdling children or children who get off task easily. ("You only have to do this one page if it is done before the timer goes off.") I have also used timers to help teach time concepts and waiting, which are two very difficult things for most special needs children. ("You may choose a movie when the timer goes off in twenty minutes if you wait without any tantrums or whining.") Timers can also help children who have difficulty with independent behavior. You can set a timer for ten minutes and tell them to work on their own for that amount of time and then you will help them. As you can see, timers are very easy to use in a wide variety of ways. Get creative!

Touch

I have often been amazed at how much support a touch on the shoulder or arm can communicate to a very discouraged child. Sometimes we fail to intervene before behavior gets out of control, and we pay for it later. Often, stopping, relaxing (see above), and having a hug can head off behavior problems before they get started. This is particularly true of behavior that results from frustration or discouragement.

CHAPTER 19

Support Groups

A S YOU HAVE probably gathered, I'm a big believer in support groups for families who are schooling special needs children. As I've said before, when we acknowledge and deal with our special needs, we are more equipped to deal with the daily challenges of having and teaching a child with learning difficulties.

If there is not a home school support group in your area for special needs families, I would like to challenge you to consider starting one. I am going to explain how our support group started and how we are structured. Feel free to take these ideas or do something different that meets the needs of your community. If you do start a group (or if you are part of an on-going group), I would love to hear from you and find out what you are doing!

Our support group started with two people, so don't think you are too small. Another mother and I began by just meeting for coffee to discuss our emotional needs and pray for each other. We put the word out to the home school community that we were meeting, and we were soon joined by two other women. From there we kept steadily growing. But people come and go depending on their needs. After about a year, we set up the Independent Study Program that now exists in order for our children to be officially enrolled in a special education school. Our support group meetings then became our school meetings, although they are open to anyone, and we continue to have people attend our meetings who are not a part of the school program.

One thing that we decided early on was that a whining and complaining session didn't do anyone any good. I have always come away from a support group meeting which became a whining free-for-all more discouraged than when I went! Instead, we have structured our meetings so that there is a devotion to help us keep our perspective, and a discussion topic in which we share frustrations but also possible solutions. Many of the discussion topics have been the basis for this book! This has seemed to be a fairly successful formula, but, whatever you do, do something! I cannot tell you how much it means to me to be able to share with other teaching parents that I have had a bad day and know that they really understand what that means!

Section Three
Planning Your Program

CHAPTER 20

Key Ingredients

O KAY, NOW WE are down to the nuts and bolts! How do we structure a program that will allow us to effectively teach our special needs learners? I feel that there are three key ingredients to successfully teaching special needs children. No matter what a program looks like, it needs to be CONSISTENT, REALISTIC, and APPROPRIATE. Although the specifics of your program will differ depending on the exact needs of your child, these more general concerns are just as important. Let's take each of these ingredients and see how to plan a program that will address each one.

Consistency

More than most children, special needs learners typically need consistency and structure if they are to be successful learners. Although I have heard people say that an "unschooling" approach is good for children with learning problems, I have to say that in most cases, I disagree. Except possibly with the very mildest of learning disabilities, special needs learners will tend to flounder and be non-productive without a consistent routine. Consistency can also help address many of the resistance and passivity issues that our children have. When children with learning problems are provided with a consistent structure, it is one less thing for them to worry about and fight against. They tend to feel more in control, which can help them better control their behavior. We also must remember that most of our children will have difficulty with organization and time concepts. By giving them a consistent routine, we can help alleviate many of the fears and confusion that are often a big part of the lives of children with learning difficulties.

It is important, however, not to confuse structure with rigidity. A consistent, structured program does not mean that you have to watch the clock and have math at 9:30 every day. The key for most children with learning problems is some kind of consistent routine so that they will know what is coming next and about how long it will take. We have a different schedule for almost every day of the week. For my daughter, the key is that she can anticipate what will happen each day. When she was still home schooling, she knew that certain things could not happen until we did our school work. This was the time that I spent with her each day on structured tasks. Although you can certainly teach many things environmentally throughout the day, I believe that children in general, but especially children with learning problems, need a consistent routine of sitting down to do some kind of structured work on a daily basis.

Consistency also involves being consistent in our standards and expectations. It is very important to remember that children with learning difficulties are rarely internally motivated to learn.

We have to be very specific in setting the guidelines for learning. For the most part, these are not the children who learn about something because it sounds interesting. There are exceptions, of course. Many mildly learning-disabled students do excel in the areas not affected by their specific disability and will be self-motivated in those areas. And many children on the higher end of the autism spectrum have specific areas of interest that they pursue (although this can be a problem in itself since they often fight learning about anything other than their area of interest!). However, in the areas where interference makes learning difficult most children will be resistant. Now, by setting clear expectations, we are not trying to be mean or oppressive! We can do many things to make learning less painful for our children, while still making sure that we communicate to them a standard for their work.

We also need to be consistent with our materials. It is tempting to switch materials whenever we see something new. We are all looking for that magic curriculum that doesn't exist! However, being consistent is better for our children than constantly switching books or methods. Of course, sometimes a certain thing that we are doing no longer works, and then it is appropriate to switch (this will be discussed later in this chapter); but we do want to be careful to give a program or method enough time to work before we make changes. In general, I like to see something used for six months to a year before we decide it's not working.

Realistic

The programs that we plan for our children must also be realistic. Realistic planning involves the same elements of scheduling, expectations, and materials.

Realistic scheduling will look very different for each family as you take into consideration the specific difficulties of your child, your other children and their needs, and any special circumstances that your family may have. You are a unique family, and the beauty of home schooling is that you can make a schedule that accommodates your needs. If your schedule doesn't match Susie Q. Homeschooler's down the street, don't worry about it. For example, for many years we schooled all year around because I believe that it is better for special needs children. I also liked the ability to take days off when I felt we needed them. Because of my work, this was less stressful for me. However, for some families, I know this isn't feasible. Some of them have other children in schools with traditional summer vacations, and it would be hard to make one child continue with school while the rest are off. Other families I know could school all year, but the mother works better if she has a long break to regroup and plan for the next year. Whatever the reasons, you need to choose the type of school calendar that realistically fits you and your child's needs. I would like to interject some ideas here, however, if you are schooling for nine months, to help keep you from losing ground over the summer.

1. Try using computer games to reinforce basic skills, such as math. Some reviews will be found in the section on Choosing Curriculum.

2. Have a daily reading period that all of your children participate in. Then your special needs learner won't feel singled out. You may want to have your other children read on their own elsewhere in the house while your child with the learning difficulties reads out-loud to you.

3. Use the summer for those hands-on projects that we know are good for our special learners, but that we sometimes feel are hard to fit in since the "basics" take so long.

4. Use the summer for field trips—same reason as #3.

5. No matter what you do during the time you take off, remember home schooling is inclusive schooling. Be on the lookout for those teachable moments, and document the things you do. That way you may get a jump on your required number of school days for next year.

Another aspect of realistic scheduling is creating a daily schedule that will both get a reasonable amount of work done and not make everyone crazy at the same time. I have people tell me all the time that it takes their children three to four hours to complete a math assignment, and by the end almost everyone is in tears. I would be, too! I don't believe it is realistic to expect any child to work at something for three hours without tears! Although every situation is different, let me give you some of the general guidelines I use in helping people plan a realistic daily schedule.

First, you may not be able to do everything every day. I found it helpful with my daughter to pick just three specific tasks I wanted her to work on in a given day and concentrate our time and energy on those. This is where your Individualized Education Plan (which we will discuss in more detail later) can be especially helpful. Pick out a few of your short-term goals each week to zero in on. Always remember that in a typical classroom, although there may be time spent on each subject each day, some of it may only be introductory work or a homework assignment!

When I taught English, I had a different activity planned for each day. On Mondays we introduced spelling and writing assignments for the week, on Tuesdays we did grammar, Wednesdays were reading days (usually discussing a reading assignment from the previous night), and catch-up. If we were doing a Literature Unit, the schedule was changed to accommodate more time for class discussions and in-class reading. So you can see that in a typical week, although we covered everything, it was spread out. Now this particular type of schedule may not work for you. I'm just giving this as an example so you can see that if you do grammar only once a week, that's okay!

Secondly, you may need to adjust the amount of work your child does. This is especially true if you have a child with a processing disability or a child who is a slow learner. It is unfair to a child who cannot work at a normal rate of speed to expect that he do a "normal" amount of work.

When I was teaching special education in a school system, I worked out with each teacher who had my therapy students how much time was reasonable for an average child to complete a typical assignment in his/her class. I would then have my special education students work for that amount of time and no more (unless they were not working). At home, you can still figure out what is a reasonable amount of time to spend by looking around your home school group for children of the same age who you consider to be average and finding out how long it takes them to do a typical math or spelling page. Then set your child's time requirements along these same lines.

As a general rule, I consider any longer than twenty to thirty minutes on one page (of something like math or spelling) to be excessive. However, if the issue is resistance, then I'm like a wall. Simply finishing the task becomes more important than the time involved, if we are dealing with a battle of the wills! Of course, we do have to make some special considerations for ADD issues. For children with true attention problems, we want to look at overall time, but perhaps we would let them work for ten minutes, get up and walk around and then come back and work ten more minutes. Whatever we find that works, the time spent working should be just that—time spent in actual work, not time in resistance or dawdling or complaining.

Realistic planning also includes setting realistic goals. In order to do this, we must take several things into consideration: our children's strengths, weaknesses, specific areas of disability, and overall ability. In setting up programs for our children, we must be careful to set goals that are neither too high nor too low. I have seen how both extremes can be harmful for children, and sources of frustration and discouragement for parents. When we set goals or requirements that are too low, it is easy to feed our children's natural resistance. However, goals and expectations that are too high create frustration and low self-esteem.

A good example of this involves children who fall in the slow learner to borderline range. Very often I see children with IQ scores falling in the 70's, whose academic functioning is also falling in the 70's to 80's. Yet these children are "significantly behind" if we look at grade levels. So everyone panics and thinks that working harder will help this child. Wrong. Look at it this way. If I have the intellectual potential to achieve at a level of for instance, a 75 standard score, and I'm making scores of 81, 78, and 55, then there is definitely room for improvement in the subject in which I scored a 55; but in the other subjects I am doing the best that I can. Give me a break (and how about a little praise!)! For children like this, it is a matter of maintaining their skills, helping them learn at their own pace, and making sure they can function in a job situation. Apprenticeship programs may be the most realistic (and appropriate) type of schooling to pursue as these children get older.

Testing can often help us in pinpointing exactly where our children are functioning and what next steps (either developmentally or academically) need to be taken. In this way, when we know where we are and where we are headed, we can be sure that our programs are realistic (see the section on Testing and Setting Your Goals for more specifics in these areas).

Realistic planning also means that we are realistic in choosing materials. First, we recognize that no curriculum or book is going to magically solve our children's learning problems. Second, we remember that "Too much of a good thing is still too much"! One mother in our support group shared that when she first began home schooling she bought several different reading programs because they all looked good in different ways. When she showed them to her son and told him they were going to work in all of them, he panicked! This may sound funny, but it is very easy to do! There are many good programs and books out there, but, realistically, we can only use one thing at a time effectively. Realistic planning includes narrowing our focus, choosing one thing and sticking with it (now we're back to consistency!).

Appropriate

Appropriate planning means that we select the level of work that is right for each child and that we use methods and materials that are right for that child, whether they are the "in" methods or not. Appropriate planning also takes into consideration when we begin working on certain things and when we stop.

Let's first talk about *when* we begin working with a child we suspect has disabilities, as this is a question I am asked all the time. In general, I am an advocate of "early intervention," meaning that I would rather do some structured work with a child as soon as I suspect a problem, than regret later that I didn't do something earlier. I especially advocate working on some structured tasks with young children when there is evidence of either a severe language problem or more severe disabilities, such as retardation, autism, or other developmental disabilities.

My daughter, for example, has been in language therapy and occupational therapy, and I have worked with her myself since age two (not to mention the three years she spent in a severely handicapped preschool program). My decision was based on the fact that autistic children tend to spend their time meaninglessly unless they are given some kind of structure and focus. The only thing she ever asked to do was watch TV, and she did not play normally until she was over six years old. So I used an early intervention model to provide her with stimulation and meaningful activity. In contrast, I have known families who did not work in any structured way with their young, delayed children because they felt it was more important to let them develop at their own pace. It keeps coming back to the same thing—you are the expert when it comes to your child. Don't ever let anyone, no matter what his or her credentials, talk you into something that you don't feel is best for your child.

Other than that, I think most children need to play; they need to be read to, they need to learn about the world around them by taking walks, and they need to be talked to a lot. If your child is not developing normally, you just do all of these things in a more structured way. If your child is slow to develop and is not showing an interest or aptitude for academics much before eight that is not necessarily reason to panic. Many studies have been done that show that children who learn to read early don't necessarily remain better readers than those who learn to read later. Of course, if a child is ready, I'm all for going ahead with academics. My youngest daughter asked to learn to read at age four and at five could do two-step addition on the computer just because she was interested.

The other aspect of appropriate planning has to do with how we teach our children. There are many possible methods that can be used to teach children with special learning needs. Some specific ideas for teaching resistant and passive learners have already been addressed under Behavior Problems. More methods for appropriately modifying programs will be discussed in the sections on Choosing Curriculum and Choosing Teaching Methods. What I would like to say here is that we must look at our own children and make decisions on the most appropriate way to teach based on their needs and abilities, not on what is popular or "best" by someone else's arbitrary standards. I cannot stress enough the fact that we know our children best. We must not be bullied into teaching our children in a way that isn't appropriate, simply because someone else tells us that this is "The Way."

Now, let's balance that last statement with a little common sense! It is wise to explore different methods and ideas and to listen to other people's ideas and experiences. For example, I have had people come to me for consultation who were adamant that phonics was the only way to teach reading but who listened when I explained why I thought a sight approach would be helpful for their child. I have seen how some parents have taken my advice and modified it to fit their own ideas about teaching and the needs of their child. They have come up with some very unique and successful programs that are not exactly what I would have designed, but they have been appropriate for the needs of their family!

Appropriate planning and scheduling also involves being flexible enough to make changes when changes are needed. It might be that it is appropriate on a given day to change our schedule to deal with behavior problems or because everyone needs a break so we sit by the fire doing oral reading all day. On the other hand, it may be appropriate to change materials or methods if something isn't working (as long as we've given it time to work and we're not just jumping from curriculum to curriculum each month).

It can definitely be a challenge to plan consistent, realistic, and appropriate programs for our children, but the rewards are enormous as our special learners begin to make progress, many for the first time in their "school career"!

CHAPTER 21

The Individualized Home Education Plan (IHEP)

NOW THAT WE have discussed the general considerations of planning a program, we turn to determining
and addressing the exact needs of your child. I recommend
that you document the specifics of your program with an
Individualized Home Education Plan (IHEP). The IHEP is
your written plan for addressing the areas of disability and/
or academic deficits your child has, and it should contain the
following information:

Current Ability: The grade level or age level your child has
achieved in each academic or developmental area. This information is gained through either your observations or testing or a
combination of the two.

Goals: Both annual and short-term goals for addressing each
area of weakness.

Methods and Materials: What you are going to use (materials)
and how you are going to use them (methods) for achieving
your goals.

Evaluations: A place to write out your evaluations of progress and continuing difficulties. I recommend that you do this at least four times per year at the end of each quarter.

The final sections of this book will take you through the process of using test scores or observation to determine where your child is functioning, setting goals, choosing methods and choosing curriculum. Once you have worked through these sections and have made your goals and chosen how you are going to address them, writing everything down in the IHEP gives you an organized way of staying focused on your goals and documenting the progress your child is making.

There are many ways that you can write out your IHEP. I have done mine on binder paper (very fancy!) and have made up my own forms using my computer. The following page shows one type of form I have used to give you an idea of how it looks when this information is all put together.

By having a detailed IHEP, you need never worry about being called to task for home schooling a child with a special learning need. All of your documentation is right there!

RESOURCES

If you are looking for more detailed resources for putting a plan together, here are some good planners and guides.

ISEP (Individualized Student Education Plan), Sharon Wallace and Julia Hoch 714.990.0199 or 714.527.5807

The IEP Manual by Debby Mills (www.nathhan.com).

The following pages are the sample form we use in my school program:

Sample

ALMADEN VALLEY CHRISTIAN SCHOOL

INDIVIDUALIZED HOME EDUCATION PLAN

Student Mary Smith   **School Year:** 02-03

Developmental/Academic Category: Math

Present Skill Level: Has mastered 3rd grade skills in everyday work, but continues to need review to maintain consistency and memory of these skills. Has difficulty demonstrating skills in testing situations (Brigance score is mastery at 2nd grade).

Annual Goal Be able to show improvement when re-tested with the Brigance. Maintain skills currently mastered. Introduce 4th grade work.

Short Term Goals	Methods and Materials
1. Review multiplication facts. When given 10 multiplication facts, Mary will be able to compute them with 100% accuracy for divisors 1-9.	1.Math Teacher's Press Math Capsules- Level B Flash Card Review Other review/drill as needed
2. Review division facts. When given 10 division facts, Mary will be able to compute them with 100% accuracy for divisors 1-9.	2. Math Teacher's Press Math Capsules- Level B Flash Card Review Other review/drill as needed
3. Learn regrouping with addition beyond one place. By June, Mary will be able to add whole numbers of 4 digits with 3 (or fewer) regroupings at 75% accuracy.	3. Moving with Math- Level B
4. Learn regrouping with subtraction beyond one place. By June, Mary will be able to subtract whole numbers of 4 digits with 3 (or fewer) regroupings at 75% accuracy.	4. Moving with Math- Level B
5. Introduce multiplication with regrouping. By June, Mary will have been introduced to multiplying whole numbers of 2 digits x 2 digits and will be able to solve these problems with assistance.	5. Moving with Math- Level C Part 1

Home Schooling Children with Special Needs

> This page is the "back" of the IHEP form (previous page). Use it to evaluate each goal.

Name_____Mary Smith_____EVALUATION Category___Math____

1st Quarter
Goal #1 Mastery _X_ Progress___No Progress___Not Addressed ___
Goal #2 Mastery___Progress _X_No Progress___Not Addressed ___
Goal #3 Mastery ___Progress _X_No Progress___Not Addressed ___
Goal #4 Mastery___Progress ___No Progress___Not Addressed _X_
Goal #5 Mastery ___Progress ___No Progress___Not Addressed _X_

Comments: This quarter, we focused heavily on review of Mary's multiplication and division facts. She has retained the multiplication, and has almost mastered the division. Some manipulatives came in very handy. Very good work this quarter!

2nd Quarter
Goal #1 Mastery___Progress___No Progress___Not Addressed ___
Goal #2 Mastery ___Progress___No Progress___Not Addressed___
Goal #3 Mastery___Progress___No Progress___Not Addressed ___
Goal #4 Mastery___Progress___No Progress___Not Addressed ___
Goal #5 Mastery___Progress___No Progress___Not Addressed ___

Comments: _____

3th Quarter
Goal #1 Mastery ___Progress ___No Progress___Not Addressed ___
Goal #2 Mastery___Progress___No Progress___Not Addressed ___
Goal #3 Mastery___Progress___No Progress___Not Addressed ___
Goal #4 Mastery___Progress___No Progress___Not Addressed ___
Goal #5 Mastery___Progress___No Progress___Not Addressed ___

Comments: _____

4th Quarter
Goal #1 Mastery___Progress___No Progress___Not Addressed ___
Goal #2 Mastery___Progress___No Progress___Not Addressed ___
Goal #3 Mastery___Progress___No Progress___Not Addressed ___
Goal #4 Mastery___Progress___No Progress___Not Addressed ___
Goal #5 Mastery___Progress___No Progress___Not Addressed ___

Comments: _____

CHAPTER 22

Testing

USUALLY THE FIRST step in planning a program for your child will involve some kind of testing. Unfortunately, too many people have taken their children in for testing, only to be given a vague diagnosis and no help in specific program planning. They leave the clinic or school even more confused or angry than when they went in. I don't blame them! In this section, I would like to discuss when testing is appropriate, what you need to be able to glean from testing and how to find someone who will give you the specific help you need.

When to test is always a big question. I don't believe there are any hard and fast rules about testing. In general, I believe that testing should be done when parents feel they need more information about their child's development or academic progress, or any time there is a worry over whether or not a true disability exists. Some parents are very comfortable with children who are developing or learning at a slower pace, and they feel no need to gain a diagnosis or other outside help. As long as they are giving the child the amount and kind of stimulation that child needs (not just letting the child sit and watch TV all day), that's fine. But other parents I work with are concerned and want more information and another opinion. For them, testing is appropriate and can either be helpful in alleviating their fears or helping them come to a realistic view of their child's disability. In that case, too, testing can help pinpoint specific areas to work on, such as language development or motor skills.

By and large, I do not recommend testing children below age eight, except where an obvious developmental disability, such as retardation or autism, exists. Testing at young ages can often lead to a false diagnosis, because even children with no true disabilities can develop at slower or faster rates. Children typically "even out" in their developmental differences around age eight, so then testing for mild learning problems becomes more accurate. However, testing younger children can still be helpful if parents are concerned and the testing is only used to identify areas of strength and weakness in development and pre-academics. Then specific skills can be worked on.

The bottom line is that you should have testing done whenever you feel it will either help you get a better picture of your child or become more realistic about the extent of his disabilities. If you do not feel that you need testing to help you work with your child, then don't let anyone talk you into it, and don't feel guilty for waiting.

However, now we are back to the difficulty of which I first spoke. Let's say that you've decided that testing would be helpful to you, and you are now looking for someone to test your child. As I said before, many parents go looking for real help and, instead, end up with a vague or "politically correct" diagnosis, rather than any specific details of what skills the child needs or how to best teach those skills. Testing is only helpful when it does the following things:

1. helps determine exact areas of disability, such as auditory processing, visual memory, etc., and explains what those terms mean and how they impact the child's learning;
2. describes the child's best way of learning and gives specific teaching ideas; and
3. details the specific developmental or academic needs the child has and gives specific ideas for teaching those skills.

If you cannot easily find someone to provide you with the type of test interpretation I've just detailed, don't give up. A large part of my consultation work involves doing just this. People send me test results, and I "reinterpret" them from a teaching viewpoint instead of a diagnostic viewpoint. Most people who have already had testing done have all the information they need; they just need someone to help them make sense out of it! In addition to myself, there are other special education consultants working with home school families. Contact the Special Needs department at HSLDA for a list in your area (www.hslda.org).

How can you find someone who will give you helpful information without unnecessary or vague diagnoses? Well, first of all, you have to be specific when you call and talk to the person you are considering using. Tell him that you are home schooling, and go through the things that you are concerned about. Specify that you are looking for help in pinpointing exact areas of need and how to best teach your child. If the person is not willing to give you these specific kinds of help, look for someone else!

Understanding the Basics of Test Results

Understanding everything about testing and test results would require an entire college course, but there are a few basic things that are essential to know. This basic information may be helpful to those of you who already have test results and are trying to make sense out of them.

First of all, it is important to understand how test scores are reported. There are three usual scores used: grade scores, percentiles, and standard scores. Of the three, standard scores are the most helpful. A standard score is based on a scale with 100 being the middle or "average score" of the scale. Then the scores are designated as follows:

Above 121	Superior
111 – 120	Above Average
90 – 110	Average
80 – 89	Below Average
70 – 79	Borderline
Below 69	Mentally Deficient

Standard scores are helpful because they are comparable. Because they are based on a common standard, a score of 90 on one test is the same as a score of 90 on another test. In this way, you can accurately determine your child's own particular strengths and weaknesses (see next page).

Another common score is the *percentile*. The percentile simply tells how well your child did relative to other children his age or grade level. A percentile of 87 means that your child scored better than 87 percent of the other children taking this test, and that 13 percent scored better than your child. These scores are also comparable, but I think standard scores are easier to understand.

The third type of score commonly reported is the grade equivalent. A grade score of third grade means that your child made the same score as most third graders taking this same test. That doesn't necessarily mean that he is doing third grade work; just that most third graders got this same score. Of course, most third graders probably are doing third grade work, but you need to be careful to look at the specific difficulties your child had on the test (see next page) and not just assume he is at a solid third grade level because of a grade equivalent score. These scores are not comparable. That is, third grade on one test may not be the same as third grade on another test, so you can't be certain if your child is really at the same level in those two areas.

After a basic understanding of test scores, the second thing you need to have is an understanding of the tests that were given. It is important to know what each of the tests was designed to show so that you can understand the specific difficulties your child demonstrated. For example, a score on the math portion of the WRAT (Wide Range Achievement Test), and a score on the math portion of the Woodcock-Johnson Tests of Achievement tell you quite different things about your child's math ability or difficulties. First of all, the WRAT is a timed (ten minute) test of computation skills only. The Woodcock-Johnson math test covers computation with no time limit, as well as math concepts and word problems. So if a student scored higher on the Woodcock-Johnson than on the WRAT, it may have been just the time limit that was a problem (if he is a slow worker) and not his math knowledge or ability.

The person who gave the tests to your child should be able to explain briefly what each test was designed to measure, but if that is not possible, or if you are still unsure about what a particular test is telling you, plug the name of the test into Google and you will get a basic description.

The next step to understanding your child's test results is to determine his particular pattern of *strengths and weaknesses*. It is important to remember that something can be a strength even if it is a below average score, if it is a strength for your child. These strengths are important to tease out, because with some children the test results can look overwhelming (as if every area needs work), when that might not be the case. One way to look for a pattern is to look at your child's learning potential compared to his achievement. Learning potential is typically an IQ score from a test such as the WISC (Wechsler Intelligence Scale for Children). A child's IQ is the score that we would expect that they would be able to achieve academically. Scores at or above the IQ are strengths; scores below the IQ are weaknesses. Here is an example:

Test Scores for Susie Q.

WISC (Full Scale)	74
Woodcock-Johnson Achievement Tests	
Reading (Word Identification)	92
Reading (Comprehension)	85
Math (Calculation)	84
Math (Concepts)	66
Writing Skills (Spelling/Grammar)	82
Writing Skills (Sentences)	74

In this example, Susie falls into the Slow Learner range (IQ 74), which means she learns at a slow pace requiring a lot of repetition. It might be tempting to look only at her academic scores and say that, except for reading words, they are all below average and in need of work. It is true that her scores almost all fall in the below average (or lower) range, but by comparing these scores with Susie's IQ of 74, we see that she is actually doing better than we would expect her to be able to do in every subject except math concepts! Looking at the scores from this perspective gives a whole different spin to Susie's needs. Although her scores are all "below" grade level, Susie really only needs remedial help in math concepts. In the rest of her work, Susie needs to be brought along at her own pace, building on the skills she already has.

What if you don't have an IQ score to compare to the academic information? One fairly good estimation, in my experience, is to average the academic scores and assume that scores above the average are relative strengths, and scores below the average are relative weaknesses. In Susie's case, this works out well. Her average academic score is 80, so her scores in Math Concepts and Writing Sentences appear weak, and her other areas are relative strengths. This is very similar to the profile we got using IQ and achievement scores. You can do the same thing with grade scores and get a fairly accurate picture of relative strengths and weaknesses. However, I have to interject a note of caution here. The only way to know if a child has a specific learning disability, or other type of learning problem, is through diagnostic testing and having someone who has knowledge of the tests and their meanings interpret those test scores. What I am describing here is a way to get a picture of academic areas to focus on, so that you can begin setting your goals realistically and appropriately.

The final step in understanding your child's testing so that you can begin to set appropriate goals (see next section) is to determine within each area of weakness what specific types of difficulties were demonstrated. These difficulties will be the basis for your specific short-term goals in each area. Returning to the example of Susie from above, her main weak area was Math Concepts. Now you need to look at the testing to find out with which concepts she had difficulty. For example, did Susie have difficulty with almost every type of problem presented, or did she only miss the problems related to time and money? Your goals and choice of materials would be different in each case (see the sections on Setting Goals and Choosing Your Curriculum).

Using Observations Instead of Testing

For those of you who wish to determine the specific needs of your child but do not wish to pursue a diagnosis or other testing, you can do something similar to what I have just described with your own observations or with a skills checklist.

An easy way to determine areas of need with your own observations is to keep a running list of specific problem areas and then use this list to form the basis for your goals. Using a skills checklist allows you to pinpoint, in a more systematic way, skills that your child has mastered and those with which he has difficulty. Several good resources of checklists are listed below.

Resources

Individualized Assessment and Treatment for Autistic and Developmentally Disabled Children Vol II, Teaching Strategies for Parents and Professionals, Schopler, Reichler and Lansing

I have already mentioned this book a couple of times, but another area it is helpful in is planning and goal setting. Excellent skills lists help parents determine skills their child has and skills that need to be worked on. www.avcsbooks.com

Skills Evaluation for the Home School, Rebecca Avery

This is a very complete listing of expected skills from kindergarten through sixth grade. Although not intended as such, this is a nice checklist for special needs students because many skills are broken down into small steps. Because it is so complete, you could almost use this as a remedial curriculum. Another feature that I liked was the explanation of the emotional development of the child at each grade level. I think it is helpful to be reminded that first graders are typically complainers, while second graders are usually industrious! Although our children's various disabilities can interfere with their emotional development, many of these emotional characteristics will still fit, while others may fit at their developmental level. Available from Alpha Omega in the Weaver Curriculum section of their website. www.aop.com

Most states or local school districts also publish curriculum guides based on the state framework. For example, the entire California framework can be found on the CA Dept. of Education website.

CHAPTER 23

Setting Your Goals

AFTER TESTING AND/OR observing your child yourself and ascertaining the exact needs she has, the next step in creating your program is to set specific goals. There are two types of goals that are good to set: long-term goals and short-term goals. The long-term goal for each area is what you hope to accomplish for the entire school year. This can be very general, such as "Score at the third grade level on the Woodcock-Johnson Math test," or "Master basic addition facts." Your short-term goals then detail how you are going to go about meeting your annual goal.

Let's return to the example of Susie Q from the previous section in order to illustrate this process. Susie demonstrated a weakness in Math Concepts. Upon further analyzing her testing, we find that she missed all of the problems relating to time and money. In order to set goals for improving weaknesses, you need to ask yourself what small steps you need to take in order for Susie to learn these skills. This is where a detailed guide, such as *Skills Evaluation for the Home School* by Rebecca Avery (see previous section for information), is invaluable in helping you break down the steps needed to learn a skill such as telling time. Each step in learning the skill then becomes one goal toward the larger goal of mastering these concepts. In this case, these goals might look something like this:

Annual Goal: To improve score on the Woodcock-Johnson Math Concepts test by one grade level.

Short-Term Goals:

Time

1. Using a play clock, Susie will set the clock hands to appropriate times written on cards to the hour (e.g., 3:00)
2. Looking at a clock set to the hour, Susie will write and say the time correctly.
3. Same as steps 1 and 2 to the half hour.
4. Same as steps 1 and 2 to the quarter hour

Money

1. Susie will correctly identify each coin and its value.
2. Susie will correctly add coins together.
3. When given an amount (e.g., $.45), Susie will use coins to show at least three combinations that add to the correct amount.
4. Susie will make change for items under $1 (for example, when given $0.50 for an item costing $0.45, Susie will correctly give $0.05 change).

In this way, you now have a specific plan on which to focus. Obviously, you will be doing other things in math, but these are the exercises into which you will put special effort as well as review and practice.

When setting goals, it is important to remind ourselves to be realistic. Setting goals too high leads to discouragement. Likewise, goals that are vague and hard to measure make us feel that we aren't getting anywhere. It is better to have a good specific goal that was set a little too short (you can always set a new goal for the next step), than a goal that causes discouragement. Remember, goals are only tools to help keep us focused and headed in a steady direction. Make them work for you.

CHAPTER 24

Special Considerations for High School Age Students

O NE OF THE scariest phrases to many home schoolers is...high school! When we have children with special learning needs, the idea of teaching them through high school may seem daunting, but as with any other aspect of schooling our kids, when we look at it step by step (and take just one step at a time) it becomes manageable. As your children reach high school age, one of the important things to think through is your specific goals for these years and what is realistic for your child to accomplish during this time. Outlined below are the typical options available for high school, and the types of disabilities that would be more likely to fit into each category.

Full High School Diploma (College ready)

For kids with very mild learning disabilities, this can be a realistic option. There are many community colleges, as well as some four year colleges, that now have learning assistance programs for students who need to take tests orally or without time limits. There are also provisions for college entrance exams (e.g. the SAT) to be modified to accommodate students with special needs. The learning disabilities of these students need to be well documented through both testing over a period of years and specific descriptions of how each high school class has been modified and evaluated. Don't forget that you can modify your child's high school program in various ways such as working orally or requiring projects instead of tests and papers. As long as the course work is sufficient for high school standards and is well documented, these changes are fine.

I recommend that you read a good guide like Mary Scofield's *The High School Handbook* (available from CHEA of CA 562.864.2432 or www.cheaofca.org). Mary's book is a valuable resource for home educators with junior high or high school aged students. It explains graduation requirements, writing course descriptions, keeping transcripts, and more. Other resources for students contemplating college include Joni Eareckson Tada's ministry which has a listing of colleges that accept LD students. Check out their website at www.jafministries.org. A book available at most libraries is *National Colleges with Programs for Students with LD or ADD* by Peterson. Check your local library.

Basic High School Diploma

Many students with slightly more severe disabilities can meet the state requirements for a basic diploma by following the minimum course of study for high school with some modifications. For example, in California, students are required to take a certain number of years of math, English, history etc.

For students who are working below grade level, they can take remedial math or consumer math as long as the semester hours are documented and a course description is written out (use Mary Scofield's guide to help you). Check with your own state organization for guidelines on high school requirements and how they need to be documented.

A great resource if you are considering this option is the use of the Pacemaker High School curriculum. This is a complete set of textbooks written at a fourth grade reading level (some even come at the second grade reading level) but with the basic course content of a high school class. These textbooks are available through our website and catalog (www.avcsbooks.com). In some states, parents can also set their own "graduation" requirements and decide when those requirements have been satisfied.

GED

Some students, however, do not end up meeting all of the requirements for a basic diploma. For these students, studying for the GED can be a good option. Students must be eighteen to take this test which, if passed, is the equivalent of a high school diploma. There are many study books on the market to help prepare for this test, and junior colleges often offer GED preparation courses. Registration for this test is done through your county office of education.

Vocational/Apprenticeship Training

Technically, apprenticeship applies to post-high school on the job training, and vocational programs indicate that job related skills are being learned during high school in addition to a basic academic course of study. Some vocational centers accept students from private schools, which should include home schooled students. Check the requirements with your own school district. You can also design your own vocational course by writing out a course description and assigning criteria for passing (see *The High School Handbook* mentioned previously for help in this area). If you have your own home based business or if you have friends with home businesses who are willing to help your child learn job skills, this can be a great option. We have also had students who have used volunteer opportunities to gain job skills and experience. Some of our students have also started businesses of their own!

No Diploma

Although this may sound sacrilegious, there are many kids who will not be able to earn a high school diploma or equivalent. These students will simply stop doing school when they reach eighteen or twenty-one (whatever you deem appropriate). This applies to kids who may be doing vocational work without completing the minimum academic requirements, and to students who are not capable of completing enough basic requirements for graduation. My daughter with autism falls into this group. She will likely live in our home until she goes to live with one of her siblings when we can no longer care for her. This doesn't mean that she will sit around and watch TV for the rest of her life. Kids with severe disabilities can be trained in basic household and job skills. Some are capable of holding jobs outside the home (McDonald's is one company with a specific commitment to hiring mentally retarded people), and others may work at home (but we know there is no shame in that!). Alison has learned basic household work which she does as part of her daily routine.

If you have a child who falls into this last group, you really need to check out The *IEP Manual* by Debby Mills (www.nathhan.com). Debby is the mother of a grown son with mental retardation. The introduction to her planner discusses a variety of important issues to consider for older severely handicapped children, and the planner itself has some particularly nice features created with more severe students in mind.

Conservatorship

Another issue that those of us with severe children may need to address is conservatorship after age eighteen. We did decide to pursue a conservatorship for our daughter primarily so that there would be no issue regarding medical decision making. Usually, a child has to be evaluated by the Regional Center in order for a court to consider a Conservatorship. If your family has not been involved with your Regional Center it may feel a little intimidating, but we found them kind and helpful. Contact a lawyer who works with conservatorships in order to be as informed as possible about this option.

Whatever you decide to pursue during and after your child's high school years, remember to submit your plans to the Lord and take it one step at a time. If you ever feel like you can't do it, think back to how you felt when they started kindergarten. See, you can do it after all!

CHAPTER 25

Understanding Learning Styles

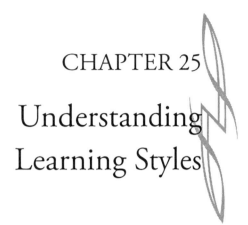

UNDERSTANDING THE LEARNING style of each of our children can be very helpful when it comes to choosing appropriate methods and materials. However, when a child has some kind of learning difficulty, his learning style becomes more crucial for us to understand as we seek to make information accessible for a struggling child. In addition, it is important to understand the limitations of learning styles so that we don't go overboard with them. First of all, let's take a look at the different learning styles and their uses and limitations for most people. Then, we will look at how learning difficulties impact learning styles and how to use this information in your teaching.

Learning styles have been defined in a lot of different ways. The two ways that I think are the most helpful are the ideas of learning modalities and learning temperament. I think that these two ways of looking at learning styles go together very well and can help us understand many different aspects of our children.

Let me give a brief definition of each idea, and summarize the major characteristics of each learning type.

Learning Modality

This is the sense through which we prefer to receive information. There are three modalities:

Auditory

This person learns best when information is presented orally.

Visual

This person learns best when information is presented visually.

Tactile/Kinesthetic

This person learns best when information is presented in a hands-on demonstration format.

An easy way to determine a difference between an auditory or visual preference is to dictate a string of eight numbers and see how many your child can repeat back to you. Then show a list of eight numbers for eight seconds and see how many he can repeat when the list is removed. If there is a difference, you can see his preference. If there is no difference you may have a tactile/kinesthetic child or a child without a strong modality preference.

Learning Temperament

This is our learning personality, how we like to approach and organize information and general strengths and weaknesses in learning. There are four common temperaments: (The following characteristics are adapted from Cathy Duffy's *Christian Home Educators Curriculum Manual, Elementary Grades.*)

Spontaneous Learner

Personality: impulsive, active, likes to be in control

Strengths: does best with hands-on/physical activities, variety and visual aids

Weaknesses: does poorly with paper/pencil tasks, poor study habits, lacks self-discipline

Routine Learner

Personality: structured, organized, responsible, needs approval

Strengths: does best with consistent, structured routine, textbook/workbook approach

Weaknesses: resists change, has difficulty with creativity, thinking skills

Specific Learner

Personality: analytical, self-motivated, likes to be in control

Strengths: oral discussion, independent work, problem solving

Weaknesses: social skills, doesn't like paper work or review

Global Learner

Personality: sociable, over-achievers, vulnerable to criticism

Strengths: creativity, conceptual understanding, enthusiasm

Weaknesses: attention to detail, perseverance, follow-through

Determining your child's learning temperament is really a matter of good observation. Chances are you can put each of your children into one of these categories just by reading these few characteristics. For more detailed lists of characteristics, see Cathy Duffy's Curriculum Manual (she also lists additional resources on learning styles).

A few important limitations to learning styles need to be kept in mind. First, almost all children under age eight are spontaneous kinesthetic learners. Second, learning styles can change—especially in children who outgrow spontaneous and/ or kinesthetic learning preferences—so don't get locked into a label. Reassess your child from time to time and see if the style you think they prefer still applies. Third, remember that your learning style is also your teaching style. If you are continually conflicting with one of your children, you may have very opposite styles. Take a look and see if you might need to do a few things that aren't the most comfortable for you in order to accommodate (within reason of course) the preferences of your child. Finally, remember that no one fits into these categories perfectly. This is a tool for you to use in your planning and teaching. Nothing more, nothing less.

Now let's look at an example of using this information in a teaching situation. Let me use myself as an example. I am an auditory, global learner. I prefer to have information presented orally and I prefer to respond orally (rather than in writing). I like the big picture over details, and often skim printed material for the main ideas. I understand concepts and ideas easily, and I dislike having to review material I already know. I like new projects, but have a hard time following through once the newness wears off. If I'm not careful, I can leave a lot of half-finished projects lying around!

If you were my teacher and you wanted to use this information to help me learn new concepts, you would remember to give me an oral overview of the material you wanted to teach so that I got a sense of the big picture. You might then assign some reading and a project, but you would be careful to give me specific short-term deadlines to help me with my weak follow-through. You might allow me to give an oral or creative presentation rather than a test or written assignment.

Although this would be an ideal situation for someone with my learning characteristics, life can't always be ideal. After all, some things just require memorization of details and detailed written work. Can I do those things? Yes, of course. Are they my preference? No. Although we all have preferences for how we like to take in and organize new information, we can use other senses or skills that are not our strongest. Writing is a good example of this for me. Even though I could stand up at a moment's notice and give you a detailed oral presentation of all the material in this chapter, it has taken me several days to get it down on paper. When I have an article or other written work to do, I know that I need to allot myself the time that it will take and I have to exercise some self-discipline to get it done as well!

Now, how do learning disabilities fit in here, and how can understanding learning styles help us in teaching our special needs learners? First of all, learning problems tend to magnify all of the characteristics of a particular learner. The strengths are magnified to be sure, but the weaknesses seem to become magnified out of proportion! In addition, even though the rest of us can use our weaker avenues of learning, children with learning disabilities often cannot learn through their weaker modalities because of perceptual or processing difficulties that make these systems ineffective.

Let me use my daughter Alison as the example here. Alison is a visual, routine learner. She is also autistic. Because of this, the strength and weakness profile of the routine learner is intensely magnified. Not only does Alison do better with a structured, consistent routine, she almost falls to pieces without it. And not only is she resistant to change, but even small (to you or me insignificant) changes can cause a major crisis in our house! Alison is a highly visual learner, but unlike a visual learner without a disability, purely auditory information is almost useless to her until it becomes familiar (routine). Therefore, her school time is rather structured and the materials I use to introduce new concepts have a lot of pictures. I use only very familiar materials to work in weak areas such as phonics (auditory perception).

Learning problems basically limit the number of ways we can present information in a meaningful, accessible way. That is why understanding learning styles and the impact of their particular disabilities can be so helpful for the child with learning problems. This limitation is one reason that children with learning problems tend to learn at an overall slower rate and require so much repetition. It is also why multi-sensory teaching techniques are usually stressed for children with learning problems. When we use multi-sensory techniques we can be sure that the stronger modality will always be in use to aid learning, but the weaker modalities will also be stimulated and therefore strengthened.

Determining the learning style of a child with a learning disability is really only a little more complicated than with any other child. It is a matter of understanding the types of learning interferences your child has (this is usually where testing can be very helpful) and observing which characteristics your child displays predominately when learning. To be sure, the characteristics may be magnified and some of the strengths may not be present (or readily observable), but the major temperaments and modality preferences should be fairly apparent with good observation.

Understanding learning styles does not mean that you can always make learning new material easy for your child. It does mean, however, that you have a better chance of making learning meaningful, accessible, and less frustrating.

CHAPTER 26

Choosing Teaching
Methods and Techniques

ASIDE FROM choosing appropriate books and materials for our children, there are specific methods or techniques that will be more appropriate or helpful than others. Some of these methods may be used in conjunction with other things, some might be used alone. Most of these ideas have been mentioned or discussed previously, but they are presented here again with definitions and examples for quick reference.

One very important thing to keep in mind when trying any new technique (or any new curriculum, therapy, etc.) is that we need to give it time before we decide it's not helping. I often consult with people and give them ideas to try, and they call me back two weeks later and tell me that "nothing's working." We have to give any new idea a good trial before we decide it's not working. When we try new methods with our children, we often get an initially good response (just because it is different); but then their natural tendency to be resistant surfaces, and they will often fight harder against the change.

On the other hand, it is important to know when a particular method or technique really isn't working so that you can make appropriate changes. Sometimes a certain thing will work for awhile, and then it loses its effectiveness. It is appropriate to make changes when this occurs. We just need to be careful that we are giving things enough time before we start making changes. Too many changes, or changing too often, is not good; but if something has become truly ineffective, then change is in order. We went through this with our daughter with some of the therapies we used. For example, we decided to use occupational therapy to assist her in developing motor skills, balance, and less sensitivity to the environment. After a year of therapy, however, she suddenly became very resistant and cried each time we went for therapy. After discussing the situation with her therapist, we determined that she wasn't having difficulty with the tasks (in fact, they were doing things she had been previously enjoying) and had made good progress, so we decided she was probably tired of the therapy and that it was time to let it go for awhile. This was appropriate because she had been at it for a good amount of time and we made a change when it was no longer working effectively.

Now we will take a look at a variety of methods and techniques. They are listed alphabetically.

Active Learning

Many special needs students are passive learners who must be taught to be active participants in the learning process. When this is the case, it is important to set aside specific curriculum time to teach active learning and thinking skills. One way to do this is to simply explain to the student that remembering something requires "brain power," and that we have to "turn our brain on" in order to remember and use anything we have learned. I have seen very simple explanations such as this help passive students understand for the first time that just because information didn't automatically "pop" into their heads didn't mean they didn't *know* it! Good resources for teaching memory techniques can be found at LinguiSystems (www.linguisystems.com).

Computer-Assisted Learning

Computers can be a great help for teaching special needs children. For children with motor-control difficulties, typing does not seem to be as difficult for them as writing, so they can express themselves with less interference from the motor system. Computer programs can also offer more interaction and visual input than many traditional forms of learning, which can be helpful for children with attention difficulties, as well as passive or resistant learners. Good programs offer immediate feedback and correction as well as self-paced learning. Two good computer curricula are Switched-On-Schoolhouse (www.aop.com) and Time 4 Learning (www.time4learning.com).

Encouragement

This may not seem like a teaching method, but encouragement can set a tone that allows more learning to take place. Although we all desire to encourage our children, I have learned that we are often discouraging to our children when we mean to be encouraging. Statements such as "I know you can do better" when a child is working as hard as he can are intended as encouragement but can actually make a child feel that we don't see or understand how hard he is trying. Encouragement is such a powerful tool that we want to be sure we are truly encouraging our children. Some ways to do this are: 1) point out what your child did correctly instead of incorrectly, and 2) acknowledge hard work, not just product.

One book that really opened my eyes to many of the ways that we can be subtly discouraging was *The Power of a Parent's Words* by Norman Wright.

"Envelope of Language" (Verbal Labeling)

Although we don't mean to, it is a fact that if we have children with language and/or communication difficulties we naturally talk to them less. Because they may not initiate conversation, it is easy to neglect to talk to them as fully as we do our other children. I know this has been true for me and my non-verbal daughter. We can be silent together for a very long time! And, although, as any mother can relate, this can be nice sometimes, the problem is that language develops and improves through hearing and using it.

This method of teaching children with language difficulties basically involves talking to them, but in a very structured way. The reason it is called the Language Envelope is because we literally surround the child with language. Sometimes this is also called Verbal Labeling because we describe everything that is being done.

Let me give an example of getting a child dressed. For a child with a very severe language difficulty, the labeling is like a monolog and might sound something like this: "Here are your clothes. First, we put on your underwear. These are pretty pink underpants. What color is this? That's right, they are pink. Okay, left foot, now right foot. Good job! What's next? That's right, your pants. What color are these pants? Good job. They are blue! Which foot are you putting in first? That's your left foot. Now your right foot. What is this? Your shirt. Here it goes over your head! Now your right arm, and now your left arm... etc." Does this sound like what we do with babies? BINGO! We naturally label the environment for babies and tell them everything we are doing, but this tendency decreases over time. If we have a child with a language delay or disorder, we have to keep this labeling going far beyond the "normal" time. This can be rather exhausting! However, I've used this technique with my daughter, and it is really helpful in building concepts, vocabulary, and awareness.

Environmental Teaching (Informal Teaching)

Environmental teaching is anything you do in its natural environment—that is, without a textbook or curriculum. Examples of informal teaching include discussing math while cooking, discussing nature while gardening or walking, learning to count by getting the forks out to set the table, etc., etc., etc.! Environmental teaching is teaching while you live and go about your normal tasks. This type of teaching can be enormously helpful to children who have difficulty connecting what they learn in a book to "real life." It can also help resistant learners because it doesn't feel like school.

Field Trips

Personally, I have always found field trips tough because of my daughter's unpredictable behavior. However, I also know how important it is for her to experience things firsthand in order to fully understand them. I have found a few things that have made field trips easier for me. First, I try to go with small groups of only one or two other families. Second, I try to go places on "off" days when it won't be so crowded. Finally, I have my "secret field-trip weapon," my mother! I often take her along as an extra hand so that one of us can be helping Alison while the other interacts with my other children and helps them enjoy their field trip experience.

Interest-Directed Learning

The phrases interest-directed or delight-directed learning often conjure up images of super-smart children off doing independent research projects. For those of us with challenged children, it's easy to think, "Yeah, right. My child can't do anything without me sitting right there with him. Projects just mean more work for me, and I'm at my limit as it is." But interest-directed learning is more than just projects or research. Interests are powerful forces that need to be uncovered and used for all students, challenged or not. And, in fact, it is even more important for children with learning difficulties that we tap their interests because the learning process is often so difficult for them.

How can we effectively use our children's interests to enhance their learning? Often, when I talk about using interests, I get several objections from parents. Let me address the most common objections I hear and share some solutions that have worked for me.

The most common objection I hear is that tapping and using interests is too much work. It is true that in using our children's interests we may have to be more creative, and we may have to stray from the "traditional" education materials that are sometimes so dear to us. Of course, it is easier to use that packaged program or the workbook series, and these are not bad things. For some things we will want to stick to a more systematic program, but it is good to veer away from the mundane to help our children learn without it always being painful (for them and for us!). Ask yourself if you would rather have a little more work or, as I typically hear, daily resistance and tears. As I taught my daughter, and as I work with other families, I have come to see this as an obedience issue. Our obedience. If God has truly called us to teach our challenged child at home (and let's be real here, how many of us would be doing this if we didn't feel it was God's call?), then we will not always be able to get by with the most comfortable way. Instead, we often have to make the sacrifice to do what is best for our children.

Tapping our children's interests doesn't have to involve big, elaborate projects. We can simply read about things that interest them, using library books, or go to places that interest them. My daughter likes snakes and lizards, so a trip to the local pet store would become a field trip. Not so, you say? Well, let's look at a simple field trip like this more closely. First of all, my daughter has many behavioral difficulties because of her autism, so virtually any trip out of the house gives us a chance to work on appropriate public behavior. When looking at the animals, we practice signing vocabulary and language expansion (that's a fancy way to say that we practice using descriptive words and longer phrases to talk about what we are seeing). When using a trip like this, we do have to take the initiative to engage our children in conversation that will promote learning and thinking. Is that more work? Sure, but well worth it.

The next most common objection I hear is the concern that if they veer off the "set" curriculum into their children's interests, vital information or skills will be left out or skipped. But using interests isn't "instead of" but rather one avenue of teaching those same skills and information.

It has been my experience that home schoolers are way too hard on themselves. Many people I work with, while convinced that they should be home schooling, still worry that there is something "magical" that special education teachers know or do that they, the parents, are missing. However, my own experience as a special education teacher is that there is nothing magical going on. In the best special education rooms I've seen, there is just good teaching occurring—systematic teaching of the basics combined with projects done in much the same way as many home schoolers, but without the individualization the child can be given at home. And in the worst special education rooms I've seen, children are being taught basic skills by rote, with little or no regard to making the task of learning meaningful or enjoyable.

I think that we have to somewhat broaden our definition of learning. Basic skills, such as math and reading, do need to be taught in a systematic way (especially for children with learning difficulties). But just because we are using a systematic math program, doesn't mean that we can't incorporate a cooking day and have a meaningful, but fun, math lesson. Our most important educational objective should be to give our children a curiosity about the world and the ability to learn. If we do happen to miss something, it can be picked up later. There is really no rhyme or reason as to why things in science or history are taught when they are anyway.

Also, depending on the level of our children's handicaps, many of us will be working on basic skills, one way or another, for years! Get a good developmental skills chart or scope and sequence, and then don't be afraid to veer away from it to make our children's learning more enjoyable. We can always come back to the basics; but once a child hates the learning process, he will be harder to teach, no matter what you do.

Another objection that I hear is that some children don't have any real interests. I hear this from parents who have either very discouraged, unmotivated students or children who fall into the more severely handicapped categories.

Sometimes we have to become detective-like as parents of poorly motivated or severely handicapped children. For example, autistic children often have limited, or sometimes rather strange, interests. When teaching my daughter her colors, I used all the great educational blocks, discs, pegs, etc., in my arsenal, but nothing seemed to hold her interest long enough to make an impact. Finally, I realized that the thing she was interested in was looking at picture books. So one day I got out Peter Rabbit and, instead of just reading the story, I stopped and pointed out the various colors in the illustrations as we read. Well, it turned out that while she didn't care a bit about all of my cute educational toys, she apparently cared quite a lot that Peter Rabbit's jacket was blue! From this simple start, I was able to use picture books with her to teach, not only her colors, but numbers, letters, vocabulary, and many basic concepts. We counted objects in the pictures to practice answering "how many?" we finger spelled the titles and reviewed letters; we used the pictures throughout each book to learn new signs or review vocabulary and to practice answering questions. In short, I did as much as I could think of with each book or picture (sometimes including acting out a part of the story). Now I realize that this example is very basic, and you may be working with a child at a much higher skill level; but the principle is the same. Find the thing that interests your child and use it to create a learning experience. Even poorly motivated or severely handicapped children are interested in something!

A final objection comes from parents of higher functioning autism spectrum children who often have intense interests—but resist learning or working on anything else! These parents worry that if they use their child's interest they will be "feeding the tiger!" I absolutely agree that with these children we need to be more careful about using their interests. We do have to make it clear that other things do have to be learned. But interests can still be used as a reward for other work. For example, if a particular animal or historical time period is an obsessive interest, reading about these things can be done each day after other work is done. They may not love the other work—in fact they may argue about it relentlessly—but making a schedule and a "rule" about other work and then rewarding that work with time allowed for their interest can be helpful. Will you move through the rest of history or science more slowly? Probably. Oh well!

Multi-sensory Teaching

Multi-sensory teaching involves using two or more senses together when learning or practicing material. For example, something might be seen and heard at the same time (combining visual and auditory senses) or talked about and manipulated at the same time (combining visual, auditory, and touch senses), etc. The reason that multi-sensory teaching is beneficial for children with learning problems is that typically one or more of the sensory systems will be weak. By involving all the senses we do two things. First, we give the child a better chance of understanding the material because we are more apt to hit his stronger system, and, second we strengthen the weaker systems through use.

Unfortunately, "multi-sensory" is one of the current educational buzzwords that I find has some people a little confused. There is a misperception that if a program is multi-sensory, it is automatically appropriate for children with learning difficulties. However, that is not always the case. Several years ago HomeRun Reading was a popular program and was touted as being "perfect" for all learners. Although this is a very solid, multi-sensory phonics program, for a child with an auditory processing or discrimination difficulty, it could be a very frustrating program. The auditory part of the multi-sensory presentation is on tape, and even I found some of the pronunciations difficult to discriminate. There is also a lot of background noise which could be confusing for children with auditory difficulties. When looking for programs, the fact that something is multi-sensory is not enough to make it necessarily appropriate for our children. We need to look at the whole program and see how it is presented and how it is paced before deciding if it is the right type of program for our children.

Another misperception is that multi-sensory teaching has to include a lot of high-priced manipulatives or other bells and whistles. There is nothing further from the truth. Multi-sensory teaching can actually be some of the easiest teaching we do! Oral reading is multi-sensory (visual and auditory); taking a walk and looking for certain colors or flowers, etc., is multi-sensory (visual, kinesthetic); making a diagram or chart while we explain a math concept is multi-sensory (visual, auditory) and if we have the child make the chart, it is kinesthetic too! One of the easiest multi-sensory exercises to do with children who are learning to discriminate letter sounds is to take letter flash cards, spread them around on the floor and make a word like "mat." Then tell the child to change "mat" to "mad." He crawls around looking for the card that will do this, picks it up, and trades the "t" for a "d." Very easy, very multi-sensory!

"Putting In"

We are "test crazy" even when we don't give tests! Some things just need to be put in over and over without the anxiety of having to recite them from memory. Multiplication facts are a great example of this for children with memory difficulties. If you have tried having your children memorize the multiplication tables without success, stop. Give them a multiplication chart and let them learn how to do the process working the problems. Believe me, if they look up 5 x 8 enough times on the chart, it will start to sink in because the pressure of having it memorized has been removed. Spelling is another area where we may need to back off of testing and reciting rules after a time. Making a chart of the main spelling rules and generalizations and referring to it as we correct misspelled words from their written work can be more beneficial in the long run than drilling lists of unrelated words week after week. My daughter had a really hard time learning to count. This is an area in which I have done a lot of just putting in the information over and over, and she was slowly able to make some progress. For example, at one point she could touch objects one at a time but needed me to count out loud for her. I would then ask "how many" there were and she would answer with the last number I said. She really still didn't understand how to count at that point, but she was getting the idea of the process. Today (at age twenty-one), counting is still difficult for her—but she can get the right number of plates and forks to set the table—so I guess something sunk in!

Repetition and Variety

These are the key words for ninety-nine percent of special needs children when it comes to successful learning. Virtually all of our children need things taught to them repeatedly and reviewed regularly even after they "get it." However, a big part of successful learning also involves varying the materials that we use when we teach and review, so the learning is generalized and not just specific to our particular materials. My daughter, for example, had learned to read the word "dog." She could read it in all of her reading books and on flash cards I had made. She could even finger-spell it and type it on the computer (how's that for repetition and variety)! However, when I pulled out *Go, Dog, Go* and tried to have her read the title, she acted as if she had never seen the word "dog" before in her life. She was unable to generalize her learning because the "d" was capitalized and she had never seen the word written like that before. That is why it is so important to look for every opportunity to review and vary the materials and experiences that our children have. Often when I test children to document progress, they will miss test items that the mother will tell me she knows the child can do. This is a good indication that the child is not generalizing learning to new contexts. Don't despair if this happens to you when your child is tested. Take it as valuable information that you need to vary the presentation of your program more, but be sure you balance that with consistency (what a juggling act we have!).

Sensory Techniques

Some children with attention difficulties are able to attend better if they have stimulation to their sensory system in the form of movement or touch. For example, I know of one girl who is able to comprehend what she reads better if she rocks in a rocking chair while she reads rather than sitting still. Other children respond to having a massage or being held tightly just prior to attending to a task. I highly recommend the books *Sensory Integration and the Young Child* by Jean Ayres and *The Out-of-Sync Child* by Carol Stock Kranowitz if you want to learn more about using sensory techniques to enhance attention and comprehension.

Textbooks

I find that many first-year home schoolers really want to use a textbook approach because of their worries over not doing enough or not teaching the "right" things in the "right" order. These are legitimate concerns for people who are new to the idea of teaching. I remember being a first-year teacher and worrying constantly if I was on the right page in the Scope and Sequence. My second year of teaching, I don't remember ever looking at the planned curriculum sequence! But for first timers, textbooks can take a lot of the worries out of the teaching process and allow you to concentrate on actually teaching. That's the good news; unfortunately, not many special needs children are able to successfully use the textbook approach to learning. The main reason is that, typically, textbooks move quickly from concept to concept and do not provide enough variety and repetition for concepts to be thoroughly learned and retained.

One way that textbook approaches can become accessible for students with mild attention or learning disabilities is to work through the text at a reduced pace and add additional practice of each concept with workbooks or environmental review before moving on. For more disabled students, a textbook could still be used as a parent guide (to help you feel more organized), but not used directly with the student. Rather you could plan your own activities and review work based on the sequence of concepts within the text.

The two major Christian textbook companies are A Beka and Bob Jones University. Of the two, I prefer Bob Jones for use with special needs students. A Beka is an accelerated curriculum (a fourth grade text is really closer to a public school fifth grade text) and has a heavy emphasis on rote memory learning. Both of these features make it more difficult to use A Beka with learning-disabled students.

Another way that textbooks can be used successfully with older students is to use what are called "high interest/low reading level" texts. These are textbooks that have been rewritten at lower reading levels, yet provide junior and senior high school students with the information they need to pass requirements in subjects such as biology, chemistry, American history, etc. We carry the Pacemaker series of High/Low textbooks (www.avcsbooks.com).

Unit Studies

Unit studies are really very similar to interest-directed learning except that a unit study takes one theme and ties it into as many different curriculum areas as possible. So, for example, if you were studying birds for science, you might read a story about birds (e.g. *Chicken Little*), then write a story about birds, and use misspelled words from the writing as your spelling, etc. This is a good method for learning-disabled children because it helps them make connections and generalizations that so many special needs learners miss. One of the most creative unit studies I have heard of is one my friend Rhonda did on "Laundry" to help her daughter learn readiness skills, such as colors, sorting, and counting. I do, however, think that elaborate unit studies are more difficult to use as the severity of a child's disability increases, and I move more toward using interests in specific, structured contexts instead of a full-fledged unit study.

The drawback to unit studies is that they do take more work on the part of the teacher in planning and preparing, and I think it takes some confidence on the part of the parent not to worry about doing things "in order," according to the traditional textbook outlines. Some of the pre-packaged curriculums, such as KONOS and The Weaver, can help with some of the preparation and anxiety; but I usually don't recommend this approach to first-year home schoolers or to people who are planning to put their children back into a structured school setting in the future. However, for those of you looking for a way to help make learning more meaningful for mildly learning-disabled children, unit studies are a good choice.

Therapies and Therapists

There are several reasons that I believe it can be wise to incorporate an outside therapist into our home schooling programs. One reason is that it affords us a break from teaching.

I have used various outside therapies for my daughter (Language Therapy, Music Therapy, and Occupational Therapy). I don't think we need to feel guilty for wanting a break from our children. People with "normal" children want breaks—how much more do we need breaks from teaching children who may be fighting and resisting our best efforts!

Another reason an outside therapist can be helpful is if our children have a particular difficulty that needs intense work or some pushing for progress to occur. It is nice to have someone else who can be the "bad guy" when working through very difficult things.

Finally, there are some things that outside therapists can offer that are, I believe, more effective in therapy than in a home program. For example, speech therapy is something that often needs to be done by a trained speech pathologist because of his/her knowledge of the physical structure of the mouth and tongue. Music Therapy can be very helpful to many children, but I have no training in music and only limited ideas of how to use it effectively for teaching (not to mention all the really cool instruments that my daughter's therapist has!).

To find a therapist in your area, start by praying for someone who will be a good match for your child and who will support your home schooling. Then talk to friends, ask private schools where they refer students with difficulties, or look for private educational therapists or learning clinics in the phone book and ask for referrals of satisfied parents. I have found wonderful therapists for my daughter by just keeping my eyes open and asking many people for referrals. Every time we have prayed for a particular kind of therapist, God has sent the perfect person into our path. Many of the associations of therapists also make referral information available through their websites. The following list of the most common therapy approaches will give you an idea of what you might look for when thinking of using an outside therapist.

- Biofeedback Therapy (useful for ADD/ADHD, particularly)
- Learning Disability Therapy (usually intense phonics training, such as Orton-Gillingham, for students diagnosed with dyslexia)
- Music Therapy (music can make learning basic concepts more accessible for severely handicapped children or resistant learners)
- Occupational Therapy/Sensory Integration Therapy (very helpful for children with motor system and perceptual difficulties)
- Speech and Language Therapy (for language delayed/ disabled and children having articulation difficulties)
- Vision Therapy (helpful for students experiencing difficulty with eye fatigue and strain due to poor muscle function)

Moving Our Children Toward Maximum Independence

The final issue I would like to address before looking at specific curriculum is that we must push our children to do for themselves the most they can, even as we are providing the one-on-one teaching and support they so desperately need. It is sometimes a difficult balance to give aid when appropriate but also to demand that they do as much as possible on their own. This was brought home to me one day when my daughter asked to have her computer program on. Usually I sit with her while she works on it and prompt her when she appears to have difficulty processing the directions on the program. On this day, however, I was busy with something else, so I just turned it on and thought "Oh well, she can just do what she can for now." Boy was I surprised when she proceeded to type all of the letters the computer character told her to, without ever getting frustrated or looking to me for help! It was a good reminder to me that I need to make sure, and not just assume, that she still needs my help on things we have been doing for awhile.

Section Four
Choosing Curriculum

CHAPTER 27

General Considerations

IF YOU HAVE just picked up this book and have flipped right to this section, I would urge you to go back to the beginning and read through the information on disabilities and issues. However, since I can't make anyone do that, I'm going to outline again the things that I feel are important for us to know and think about before we begin choosing curriculum.

1. We need to have a thorough understanding of our children's disabilities.
2. We need to have a realistic picture of our children's unique blends of strengths and weaknesses, including overall learning potential.
3. We need to have a realistic picture of what home schooling can and can't do for our children.
4. We need to have confronted any emotional issues that are potential roadblocks to our effectiveness.

In addition to these topics, which have been covered elsewhere in the book, we now turn to the issue of being realistic about curriculum. Just as home schooling is not a magic cure for our children's learning problems, neither is there a magic curriculum that will solve all of our children's learning difficulties. With each child, there will be things that will be more appropriate than others—and that's the beauty of home schooling—we can design a completely individualized program for each child using the materials that are the most appropriate for him! But it is important to keep in mind that appropriate isn't perfect.

The other thing we must think about is the type of materials which are the most appropriate for us to teach with. There is sometimes too much guilt passed out in home schooling! A unit study may be a great way to teach, but if we are already up to your eyebrows, don't feel especially creative, and the idea of planning a unit study makes our heads swim—it won't be a great teaching tool at all. In fact, it will be a disaster! There is nothing wrong in using a good textbook if it will help us stay on track. Granted, we may need to make some modifications if we use a traditional textbook to accommodate our children's learning difficulties, but if it makes teaching more realistic in our situations, then it is fine.

Finally, we must take into consideration our children's likes and dislikes. Contrary to what we may have read before, some children just plainly like workbooks. Workbooks sometimes make children feel secure, especially those with organizational difficulties, because they know where everything is and can see that they are making progress. Some children are deeply offended if they are put into a textbook two or three grade levels below where they are "supposed" to be (textbooks might not be a good choice in this case!), while other children don't care as long as they can do the work. Some children need very specific tasks that begin and end, and some can work with open-ended projects. Some children need help or guidance with everything they do; some can be independent with work outside their areas of disability.

I'm sure you're getting the picture! You know your child best. Don't plan your program around what is "supposed to be" the best way to do things; plan it around what is appropriate for your child's needs, what is realistic for your particular family or personal teaching situation, and what kinds of materials your child will respond to best. If you do this, you will have a truly individualized education plan that will beat the socks off anything else around!

In the sections that follow, I will explain the basics of a variety of learning problems and give specific types of resources or curriculum appropriate to that difficulty. After these sections other books or curriculums that don't fit into the areas discussed will be listed. Please remember that if I don't mention a program you already have, please don't feel that you necessarily have to start over with all new materials. I am giving you my favorite materials, but there are many more that you could use or modify. Let me give you one example of what I mean. If a family comes to me with no reading program, and their child is in need of a structured, phonics approach, then I will usually recommend either *Recipe for Reading* or *At Last a Reading Method for Every Child* because I think they both are well structured, easy to use and less confusing for children with disabilities than either *Writing Road to Reading* or *Phonics for Reading and Spelling*.

However, I have many parents who come for consulting who already own either the Spaulding or Dettmer books. In that case, there is no point in spending money on a whole new program. Instead, we discuss how to simplify the program they already own to make it more accessible for their special learner. For example, both Spaulding and Dettmer recommend teaching all the sounds of each phoneme at once. This approach is usually very confusing for children with language learning problems. So I suggest that they take the same cards and teach only the first sounds for the consonants and short vowels (skip the other phonemes for now); then use the cards to teach blending by putting out a consonant card, a short vowel card, and another consonant card; and then rearrange the cards to create more short vowel words. These words (or short vowel words from the lists in the book) can then be dictated for spelling after they can be read easily. In this way children learn to read only short vowel words first (which is less confusing for most special learners), but no further purchase of materials has been necessary. They would then progress through the rules (such as adding in the idea of long vowels by teaching the silent-e) and the other phonemes at whatever pace their child could handle comfortably.

This is just one example of how a program can be modified to fit a particular child. Read through the reviews here and see what reasons I give for recommending each program. If you already have materials, ask yourself if you could do something similar. What could you do with what you have already to make it more appropriate for your child? That won't work with everything, but you may save some money if you spend a little time thinking creatively about using what you have.

Some of the general modifications that can be made to programs include the following: slowing down the pace; adding additional practice/review opportunities; skipping unnecessary review if mastery has been demonstrated; skipping concepts that are proving too difficult and returning to them later; giving students with memory difficulties aides, such as multiplication charts or spelling rules charts; allowing oral, instead of written responses; shortening assignments (for example, doing only the even numbers); breaking material into smaller steps; color-coding information with markers or colored cards; rewriting information so that the print is larger or there is more room to work (for math problems, for example); using textbooks on tape (available from Recordings for the Blind and Dyslexic—www. rfbd.org); and creating hands-on/manipulative opportunities. These are just a few general ideas. Appropriate modifications are as endless as the needs of each child and the imagination of each parent! Remember, you are the teacher, books and programs are only tools. If you don't lose sight of that important truth, you are already on your way to successfully teaching your special learner!

CHAPTER 28

Understanding and Strengthening Motor Skills

CHILDREN WHO STRUGGLE with motor skills find it difficult to effectively demonstrate what they know. This leads to an immense amount of frustration and anger if not properly addressed. Motor skills are of three types: gross motor skills, fine motor skills, and oral motor skills. In this section, I will explain the three types of motor skills, how difficulties in each area can impact learning, and methods for both strengthening and/or working around each type of difficulty.

Definitions and Impacts to Learning

Gross Motor Skills

Gross motor skills are skills involving the large muscle groups. The most obvious gross motor skills are such things as walking, running, climbing, etc. Many people associate these skills with athletic ability alone and not necessarily academics. However, children who struggle with gross motor tasks typically experience difficulties with sensory integration which is the ability to gather, coordinate, and act on data from the external (visual, auditory) and internal (balance, spatial, touch) sensory systems. Signs of sensory integration problems include clumsiness, poor balance, poor hand dominance, motor overflow movements, difficulty imitating motor sequences, and slow motor reaction times. Many people (especially occupational therapists) believe that these basic sensory skills are the building blocks for higher learning and thinking and that gross motor clumsiness (dyspraxia) should be worked on primarily to build a strong base for further learning.

Gross motor difficulties can also impact learning by either enhancing or further diminishing self-esteem. Children with learning problems who are athletically gifted can use these skills to feel better about themselves, while children who have motor problems on top of other learning problems can feel even worse about themselves.

In addition to self-esteem and sensory integration, structured work on gross motor skills can directly benefit children with social awareness and hyperactivity difficulties. By becoming more aware of their bodies in relationship to the environment and others, children with social behavior concerns can better understand personal space and appropriate social limits. Hyperactive behavior can often be managed more effectively with a structured gross motor program.

Fine Motor Skills

Fine motor skills refer to the ability to use your hands or fingers effectively. Although many people think only of handwriting when they think of fine motor skills, much more than penmanship is involved here. It will be helpful to think of fine motor skills on two different levels.

BASIC FINE MOTOR SKILLS: The most basic fine motor skills involve grasping with the hands and fingers, and using both hands together in coordinated movements. Examples of these skills would be picking up small items one at a time and putting them into a bowl or container, or opening a jar with a lid. Many children with problems at this level also do not possess adequate hand strength. The ability to use the fingers and hands in controlled ways is important in many tasks including: self-help skills (e.g. buttoning), sign language (for children with extreme language impairments), cutting skills, and scribbling (pre-handwriting skills).

VISUAL-MOTOR INTEGRATION: This next stage involves refining the basic skills into something more controlled and integrated with other perceptual information (primarily visual). Now, instead of scribbling all over a piece of paper (a fine motor skill), the ability to draw a specific shape and eventually to write letters and numbers become the primary tasks. Children with visual-motor integration difficulties are not readily able to coordinate visual information and motor output. Sometimes the difficulty can lie primarily with the visual system, but often both systems are faulty. Often, children lack efficient MOTOR MEMORY, which is the ability to recall the way a letter or number should be formed automatically and with effective speed. Children with visual-motor integration difficulties have slow, labored writing. They often fatigue easily, and have difficulty writing and thinking at the same time.

Oral Motor Skills

Oral motor skills primarily involve the ability to articulate speech clearly and accurately. Although usually a result of oral motor difficulties, any child with articulation problems should have his hearing tested to rule out a hearing loss or distortion. The types of difficulties associated with oral motor dysfunction include voice disorders, mispronunciation of single sounds (articulation), stuttering (fluency), and sound sequencing difficulties (phonology).

Oral motor difficulties do not impact learning directly, but rather make it more difficult for a child to express herself. For some children, this impacts their self-esteem and makes them more reluctant to discuss information or answer questions. Other, more severely handicapped children may not be as self-conscious about their speech, but speech problems make communicating wants and needs more difficult and increase frustration, which for many children is difficult to deal with constructively. Not only do speech difficulties make understanding a child difficult, but it can add to negative perceptions by other people. In other words, the more pronounced the articulation or other difficulties, the more "disabled" your child will appear to others.

Remedial and Compensatory Activities

Working with motor skills, as with all other academic areas, requires a balance of remedial work and compensatory activities. How heavily you lean one way or the other will depend on many factors such as the age of your child, the severity of his/ her disability, and your own personal philosophy of education. The following section outlines general ideas for both remedial and compensatory approaches.

Gross Motor

Remediating gross motor skills can involve working with an occupational therapist to shore up underlying systems to improve balance, spatial awareness, and kinesthetic systems (the foundations of sensory integration), or choosing activities that are especially designed to improve general gross motor skills. These can be found in most curriculum guides for severely handicapped children. Some of these activities may seem simplistic, but children with coordination difficulties can be very physically passive and have difficulty with even simple things like toe touches or catching a ball.

Compensatory ideas for children with gross motor difficulties might involve something as simple as avoiding sports type activities and cultivating other skills to the use of specially adapted equipment to make gross motor activities more accessible. See the list of catalogs at the end of this section.

Fine Motor

Choosing remedial activities for fine motor difficulties will depend on the type of difficulty or difficulties present. For basic fine motor difficulties, activities can range from refining the ability to use a pincher grasp by picking up small objects to intricate cutting activities. Exercises to increase hand strength are usually in order at this stage. Activities such as working with clay can improve hand strength and coordination. Choose activities that best fit your child by using a good, developmentally arranged guide such as the resources listed at the end of this chapter. If you have a child who has difficulties at this low level, remedial activities are a must. However, some compensatory tools are available through specialty catalogs. For example, special scissors are available to help children with grasping and hand strength difficulties.

Visual-motor integration difficulties cause the most "academic" type of problems because they affect handwriting legibility and speed as well as the ability to express thoughts easily through writing. It is the one area where some degree of compensation is a must because of the intense frustration that accompanies difficulties of this type. However, remedial activities are very important also, especially with younger children. As children reach junior high age and beyond, compensation for handwriting and written expression difficulties becomes more necessary and appropriate, but in younger children it is important to strengthen this area as much as possible.

Remediation activities for visual-motor integration can include: vision therapy exercises, mazes, chalkboard exercises, puzzles, tracing, copying exercises, handwriting practice and, of course, just plain old writing! The type of activities you choose and the amount of time spent on them each day will depend on your child's level of dysfunction and his/her frustration tolerance. For some children, any activity that involves a paper and pencil is painful, which is why I especially like to see remedial and compensatory approaches combined.

Compensation in this area usually takes the form of relieving the amount of writing required of the student. In general, I like to have students with motor difficulties have a set amount of written work each day (to provide some remediation) and then use either oral discussion or a computer for the rest of their work. This relieves pressure and frustration and allows students to express themselves without the interference from their motor systems.

Finally, let me make a few comments about handwriting itself. Many children with learning problems will never have really good handwriting. The key here is to find the type of writing your child can do best and go with that. Some children cannot seem to master cursive writing. For these kids, let them print. After all, you really only need to know cursive in order to sign your name, so teach them how to write at least their name in cursive. On the other hand, there are children whose printing is awful. They reverse b's and d's and other letters are completely unreadable. Surprisingly enough, many of these children do better in cursive! There is no need to wait for a certain age to begin cursive. Some programs for dyslexic children start cursive in kindergarten and never specifically teach printing. If you have a child who reverses at all, I'd give cursive a try. Of course, if writing is painful no matter what, get your kid on the computer except when you are doing "writing practice."

Oral Motor

This is one area where remediation is your only option other than doing nothing. There is no real way to compensate for mispronouncing sounds and words or stuttering except not talking! Remedial activities to strengthen and retrain the oral muscles can be done through speech therapy with home follow-up, or by working at home with the aid of a guide such as Straight Talk (see the resources at the end of this section). I personally like to have children with articulation or stuttering problems seen by a speech therapist for evaluation and initial training because they know lots of tricks for strengthening these muscles that you or I wouldn't think of by ourselves! Manuals such as Straight Talk can be great for working with your child after an initial evaluation if articulation is the only difficulty.

RESOURCES

Resources available from AVCS Books www.avcsbooks.com or our print catalog. If an item is starred (***) it is available on the website. If not, it is available in the catalog. You can request a catalog on the website.

Brain Integration Therapy: The Educational Model***
Dianne T. Craft, M.A.

This excellent book provides specific exercises to use with students who are struggling with dyslexia, handwriting, visual processing difficulties, auditory processing difficulties, and eye/hand coordination problems. We know that people who process information effectively use both sides of their brain. Children with learning disabilities, however, often only use one side of their brain efficiently which makes processing more difficult. By stimulating the neurological system with these exercises, children who have these types of difficulties can begin to use their whole brains to process information and make learning and memory more efficient and automatic.

Brain Gym*** *Paul Dennison, PhD*

For more than fifty years, pioneers in behavioral optometry and sensorimotor training have provided statistical research showing the effects of movement upon learning. Dr. Dennison's familiarity with this research, oriented mainly toward children with specific language disabilities, led him to extrapolate this information into quick, simple, task-specific movements of body and energy which are appropriate to the special needs of people learning in our modern, highly technological culture. This book was written so that people can experience the vitalizing effects of these movements in their daily-life activities.

Teaching Activities for Autistic (and Developmentally Delayed) Children***

Levels: Developmental ages birth-6 years

Appropriate for: Autistic and Developmentally Delayed children who are functioning below the 6-year-old level.

A comprehensive guide to planning programs for severely disabled children. Contains activities in imitation, perception, gross motor, fine motor, eye-hand integration, cognitive performance, cognitive verbal, self-help, and social areas. Also contains a very helpful developmental level chart to help you determine your child's functional age in each category.

I Can Write***

Appropriate for: Students with a reading level of approximately 1st grade.

This program is designed to be used with students who need repetition to aid in developing simple writing skills. It uses a fade-out technique where the student first copies only one or two words from a sentence, and is gradually led to write an entire sentence without clues. These books are excellent supplements to the Apple Tree Language program for students who need more reinforcement of sentence writing skills (see the Language section for more information on the Apple Tree Program).

Ready Writer

Level: Pre-writing

Appropriate for: Children learning to write or children with motor control or eye-hand coordination difficulties.

Some more interesting and fun material for developing pencil skills than just letter tracing. These cute pictures come with stories and are printed on good quality paper that won't tear easily under excessive pencil pressure. Each exercise is designed to help children practice the different pencil strokes needed for writing, but specific letters are not practiced until the end of the book. Twelve copies of each exercise are provided in the book for repetition and mastery.

Handwriting Program for Cursive

Appropriate for: Beginning cursive instruction

This book is part of the Preventing School Failure series and is based on the multi-sensory Orton-Gillingham teaching method. The workbooks provide large models for tracing and progress down to 1 ½" lined paper to facilitate the transition to regular writing paper.

Cursive Writing Skills

Appropriate for: Junior high and high school aged students who need work on cursive skills.

Available in separate editions for right- or left-handed students, this book has three parts: pre-writing exercises to establish correct posture, pencil grip, and paper position; practice joining letters and copying.

Handwriting Without Tears

Levels: Beginning writing skills to cursive

Appropriate for: Children learning to print or any child struggling with printing and/or cursive writing skills. Works for both right- and left-handed children.

The features of this excellent handwriting program, developed by an occupational therapist, include:

Developmentally-based learning sequence

Learning skills put into meaningful and immediate use

Built-in review of learned skills to promote mastery and fluency

Clear and consistent page and lesson formats

Comfortable transition between readiness, printing, and cursive

Valuable support to other language arts skills

How to Teach Your Child to Read and Spell Successfully
Dr. Sheldon Rappaport
This is a very informative and practical book which explains how auditory and visual processing problems impact children's ability to learn to read and spell. Dr. Rappaport gives very understandable explanations as well as simple tests and exercises to help parents determine if their child is experiencing the problems described and how these areas can be strengthened.

Other Resources

Sensory Integration and the Child by Jean Ayres

Straight Talk—A Guide to Correcting Mispronunciations www. NATTHAN.com

Right-Line Paper (paper with raised lines for kids who have trouble staying on the lines) Pro-Ed 512.451.8542 www.proedinc.com

Can Do Kids www.candokids.com Calisthenics combined with math facts—a great way to work on gross motor skills and math at the same time!

Catalogs

Flaghouse (Occupational therapy aids) 800.793.7900 www.flaghouse. com

Toys for Special Children (adaptive aids for severely motor impaired) 800.832.8697 www.enablingdevices.com

OT Ideas (scissors, pencil grips, slant boards, visual-motor training aids)

877.768.4332 www.otideas.com

Linguisystems (articulation, fluency, phonology curriculum) 800.776.4332

www.linguisystems.com

The Speech Bin (articulation, fluency curriculum) 800.850.8602 www.speechbin.com

Academic Therapy Publications (mazes, visual-motor exercises) 800.422.7249

www.academictherapy.com

CHAPTER 29

Understanding and Strengthening Reading Skills

WORKING WITH YOUR child who is having difficulty reading seems overwhelming because there is so much to do that other children pick up more or less automatically. To begin with, arm yourself with knowledge by studying the flow charts at the end of this section that detail normal reading development and reading dysfunction. Pinpoint where your child is having difficulties so that you can begin at a point that best fits your child.

The second thing to do is to relax. If your child is struggling with reading, stress (yours and/or your child's) will only make things worse.

The next thing to do is focus. To strengthen reading skills, we need to be aware of all three levels of reading and work on them simultaneously.

The three components of reading are:

1. Underlying Skills

2. Word Level Skills
3. Comprehension Skills

However, this can seem overwhelming unless we focus on only the weakest skill in each area first. The following discussion takes each area and gives suggestions for working on various aspects of reading weakness. As you read this, please keep in mind that this is a very general discussion. Each individual child will need a slightly different combination of techniques or will need a different emphasis. Some children have less disability than what I will describe here and may not need work in every area, while other children have much greater disabilities than simply reading and will need even the suggestions here to be modified. This discussion is a starting place for understanding the general idea of working with a child struggling with the reading process.

Underlying Skills

The most important perceptual skills for reading are visual. So the first thing we always want to rule out is any type of dysfunction in the eyes themselves. This is best done by a developmental optometrist who is trained to look at the entire functioning of the eyes as they relate to reading. You can screen for vision related difficulties yourself using the book, *How To Teach Your Child To Read and Spell*, by Sheldon Rappaport, but I do encourage an exam as well if difficulties are suspected.

If indicated, exercises can be used to strengthen the eyes for better functioning. There are specific exercises given in Dr. Rappaport's book, or a developmental optometrist can prescribe appropriate exercises.

Some of the most common visual difficulties that impact reading are visual discrimination and tracking skills. In addition to any exercises for the eyes themselves, practicing tracking and discrimination skills can be helpful for children who are having difficulty remembering what letters look like and/or who lose their place easily while reading. Several books by Academic Therapy Press such as *Symbol Discrimination and Sequencing, Letter Tracking and Word Tracking* are good short exercises for developing quick visual scanning skills.

After determining if the eyes are functioning properly, the next most important skill to work on is visual memory. One of the biggest problems most children with reading problems have is the inability to effortlessly recognize words that they have seen countless times. They often laboriously decode the same words over and over—sometimes even on the same page! Visual memory skills can be built through a number of simple games and exercises. Games such as concentration with a deck of cards or looking at a picture and then naming as many things in the picture after it is removed are excellent and easy ways to improve visual memory skills. Some children, however, have good visual memory for pictures, but poor visual memory for letters or words. These children need to develop "Symbol Imagery." The book *Seeing Stars* by Nanci Bell explains how to help children with this important skill.

Word Level Skills

There are two elements to this level of reading—decoding words phonetically and reading words by sight. As you can see from the flow chart of the normal reading process (pg. 219), all good readers eventually become "sight readers," but phonics is the method used to learn most new words. Unfortunately, children with reading problems do not learn and apply phonics easily. Thus, they need specialized presentations or methods for learning the sound-symbol associations of phonics. Still other children may have such severe language or cognitive impairments that learning words as wholes is easier for them. For children who learn better by sight, phonics is used to help differentiate between visually similar words.

When children are struggling with reading, it is easy to get stuck at basic phonics without a means to move on. Because this is very discouraging, I believe that a simplified, three-pronged approach gives you a more balanced program by simultaneously:

1. teaching simplified phonics
2. teaching sight words
3. emphasizing fluency in reading over word by word decoding through repeated readings

Simplified phonics means teaching only the most common sounds and rules without any exceptions until those are solidly mastered. The programs I like the best for this are *Phonics Plain and Simple, Recipe for Reading* and *At Last, a Reading Method for Every Child. Phonics Plain and Simple* is specifically designed for very young and very handicapped children and is a good place to start. The other two programs are for kids at a beginning reading level (Kindergarten/1st grade). They both stick to the basics and provide very good, simple explanations of the techniques for teaching children who need extra help mastering phonics associations. (If you already know how to teach phonics and are just looking for good material for review and reinforcement, the "Explode the Code" series is very good).

It is important to teach sight vocabulary at the same time as reviewing and practicing phonics because many poor readers spend so much time at the decoding level that they never get to experience the flow of reading. Not only is this very discouraging, but since we become better readers by reading—kids who do not make the leap from decoding to fluent reading have much less opportunity to improve their reading skills. There are several lists that can be used to drill sight vocabulary. I like the Functional Word List (the 400 most functional words) from the Brigance Test of Basic Skills. The Dolch List of 220 basic sight words is also a good list to work from (Google "Dolch word list" and you will find many versions of this list), and the *Recipe for Reading* manual has several lists of sight words. Make flash cards and drill until the words are automatic. Use the imaging techniques from *Seeing Stars* if memorizing the sight words is difficult. I would start with twenty to twenty-five words at a time and add five more each time those are fairly well mastered. (For children with more severe disabilities, you may have to cut the number of words way back.)

The final ingredient is repeated reading of material at the level where reading becomes choppy and word-by-word. The idea here is to increase reading fluency, speed, and to encourage visual reading. Allow your child to read through the selection the first time and decode any unfamiliar words. Put these on flash cards. Emphasize the fact that phonics help you figure out new words, but that once decoded, the word should be memorized as a whole. Review the new or troublesome words the next day, and then have your child read the selection again. If your child stumbles or tries to sound out the words you have already worked on, cover up the word and ask, "What do you think that word should be?" This helps him to start using context to decide what word makes sense and helps build comprehension skills. Repeat this until the selection can be read fluently at a good rate. Then proceed to the next selection.

If your child has the opposite problem, he guesses at each word based on the look without using any decoding, you will need to do the opposite! In this case, take any words your child is guessing at wildly and put them on flashcards, but have your child write the word out and say each sound as he writes. Tell him that we should use our eyes to help us read, but that we must look at the whole word and notice all the letters. Remind him that he also needs to think whether the word he said makes sense in the story he is reading. Repeat this until the selection can be read at a good rate. Then proceed to the next selection.

Comprehension Skills

It is easy to neglect comprehension skills when just the activity of reading is difficult, but by teaching comprehension skills directly we can often help our children gain reading fluency as they learn to use the context to aid in figuring out new words.

There are several different techniques for teaching comprehension skills. Probably the best overall technique is teaching kids to visualize what they are reading. Good readers naturally "make pictures in their heads" as they read. This is why good readers usually hate movies of their favorite books—it doesn't "look" the way they imagined it! Most poor readers on the other hand do not visualize. This makes comprehension much more difficult and often results in having to re-read passages several times. A great resource for teaching visualization skills for comprehension is the book *Visualizing and Verbalizing* by Nanci Bell.

A related technique is summarizing. This is usually done as part of the visualizing and verbalizing technique, but can be done on its own as well. The idea here is to simply have the child relate verbally the main idea and at least three details about a selection that he has read. If this is very difficult, then probably backing up to teaching visualization skills is in order, but for kids who can already visualize, this helps them learn how to pick out the most important information and organize it for re-telling.

Comprehension can also be compromised by poor vocabulary or sequential memory skills. My two favorite workbook series for addressing these types of comprehension difficulties are "Starting Comprehension" (K-2nd) and "Reading Comprehension in Varied Subject Matter" (2nd-12th). The upper grade books also focus on identifying main ideas, details, and inference skills.

Compensation Strategies

The final area of reading that needs to be addressed is reading for information. This is the last stage of reading, but the one which usually seems unattainable by children with severe reading problems. Because of this, children with reading problems are at risk for falling far behind in the amount of information they are able to learn compared with other children their age. While reading instruction, review, and practice are going on separately, compensation strategies should be employed to make sure this does not happen. The most common compensation strategies for reading are:

1. High/Low books. The "high" stands for "high interest," and "low" stands for "low reading level." These are

books that are written at 4th grade or lower reading levels, but with topics that will interest and inform older students.

Some examples are:
>   Pacemaker Curriculum textbooks
>   Bring the Classics to Life
>   High Noon Books

2. Read content material to your student or use books on tape when available.
3. Use videos to convey information in science, history, and literature.

Final Thoughts

Above all, if your child is struggling with reading, don't despair. Many very successful people have struggled with reading problems and have overcome them. You may want to read some biographies of these people with your child. Some examples are: Woodrow Wilson, Nelson Rockefeller, Thomas Edison, Ann Bancroft (first woman to reach the North Pole), Bruce Jenner, and Ben Carson (famous neurosurgeon). Another very good book is *The Uncommon Gift* by Jamie Evans. It is the autobiography of a dyslexic.

More than anything else, remember that your child is more than his reading problem. Work on it and work around it at the same time, but never lose sight of the fact that your child has strengths as well as weaknesses. Capitalize on those strengths and thank God for the child He has given you. Everything—even reading problems—has a purpose when put into God's hands!

Normal Process of Reading Development

Readiness Skills Acquired

Age: 6 months – 6 years

Skills such as motor development, visual perception, auditory perception, and awareness of left/right develop naturally or through minimal instruction. Beginning reading skills such as letter recognition and "pretend reading" (mimicking the reading process through imitation and memory of stories that have been read to them) develop with minimal instruction.

Decoding Skills Acquired/ Comprehension Skills Acquired

Age: 6 – 7 years

The child can only do one of these effectively at a time. Reading tends to be word-by-word. Comprehension may lag behind if only decoding accuracy is stressed. Reading skills improve as words are memorized and don't have to be decoded each time they are encountered.

Fluent Reading Achieved

Age: 7 – 8

The child decodes visually and comprehends simultaneously within a limited vocabulary, but needs to slow down and decode unfamiliar words. Usually cannot read independently to acquire new information. Comprehension skills tend to be tied to confirming existing knowledge.

Age: 9 + years

Sight vocabulary is now quite extensive. Simultaneous visual scanning and comprehension become automatic. Reading speed is varied according to the depth of comprehension needed. Decoding is limited to unknown or increasingly technical words. Child becomes able to read and gain new information. Level of reading ability catches up to and passes language found in everyday speech.

Reading Dysfunction

Readiness Stage

Skills such as motor development, visual perception, auditory perception, and awareness of left/right do not develop naturally or through minimal instruction. Many of these underlying skills have to be worked on and taught directly. Some skills may never develop fully or may need constant work (e.g. distinguishing left and right). Basic skills such as recognition of colors, shapes, numbers, and letters do not come easily and require direct instruction and clues for retention. Language, cognitive, and memory skills may also lag developmentally and may need direct intervention.

Beginning Decoding Skills/Beginning Comprehension Skills

Children with reading dysfunction are often "stuck" at this stage for an extended period of time. Perceptual interference, memory difficulties, attention problems, and language impairments can cause difficulty in acquiring basic decoding and comprehension skills. Sounds, letters, and words are often not memorized easily which leads to labored decoding and re-decoding of words. Comprehension skills are severely impacted if not taught directly and aside from decoding.

Fluent Reading Stage

The child decodes visually and comprehends simultaneously within a limited vocabulary—often significantly below grade level. Reading tends to be slow. The child may need to decode words that are not seen on a regular basis. Usually cannot read independently to acquire new information, and may not reach completely fluent reading stage. Comprehension skills tend to be tied to confirming existing knowledge.

RESOURCES

Resources available from AVCS Books (www.avcsbooks.com or our print catalog). If an item is starred (***) it is available on the website. If not, it is available in the catalog. You can request a catalog on the website.

Tracking Materials

These materials are designed to enhance visual discrimination and tracking skills for children demonstrating difficulties with letter reversals, tracking, directionality, and memory for letters—a valuable remedial resource for the struggling reader. See catalog for specific titles.

How to Teach Your Child to Read and Spell Successfully ***
By Dr. Sheldon Rappaport
This is a very informative and practical book which explains how auditory and visual processing problems impact children's ability to learn to read and spell. Dr. Rappaport gives very understandable explanations as well as simple tests and exercises to help parents determine if their child is experiencing the problems described and how these areas can be strengthened.

Basic Skills

At Last, A Reading Method for Every Child *** *by Mary Pecci, MA*

Levels: Beginning reading instruction or remedial instruction

Appropriate for: Children learning to read, children struggling with traditional reading approaches who need a simplified phonetic approach which also addresses sight words.

This is a manual which explains how children learn to read and is designed to either remediate or head off potential reading problems. Mrs. Pecci gives step by step instruction for teaching the author's simplified approach which successfully combines phonics and sight instruction in a unique way. This is not a pull off the shelf and use curriculum. It is a crash course in understanding and implementing the process of reading instruction. If you have a child who has struggled with reading and you want to know exactly why and how remedial reading instruction works— this book is for you. Very teaching involved—this is not a light weight program, but it is a winner!

Pathway Readers

Levels: 1st– 4th grade reading levels

Appropriate for: Children reading at a strong first grade level and above who need meaningful readers with a combination of phonics and sight words. Mary Pecci recommends these readers in her book "At Last a Reading Method for Every Child."

Seeing Stars: Symbol Imagery for Phonemic Awareness, Sight Words, and Spelling *by Nanci Bell* ***

This is a very helpful manual if you have a child who is struggling with the step of "putting it all together" in either reading or spelling. The concept is to teach children how to use their visual, auditory, and comprehension systems simultaneously—a huge problem for most learning disabled children. This manual is well written and easy to understand, and consistently receives high ratings from the parents using it.

Recipe for Reading

Levels: K-3rd grades and remedial

Appropriate for: Children with Specific Language Disabilities (Dyslexia), other Learning Disabilities, Slow Learners who need review of basic phonics, or any child struggling to read who is capable of learning phonics.

This is a multi-sensory phonetic reading program that was specifically developed for children with language learning disabilities. The manual provides a very easy to understand format for effectively working with children who need remedial phonics work.

Explode the Code ***

Levels: K-4th grade, remedial

Appropriate for: Children with Learning Disabilities or Language Disorders who are capable of phonics, Slow Learners, severely disabled children if used at a slow pace for practice.

A workbook series designed to help children master the basics of phonics. It has cute illustrations by other children, and plenty of practice for each phonetic element. Every unit provides practice in sound discrimination, reading words that follow a particular pattern or rule, writing the words, and comprehension. This is a thorough approach, and you can always skip some of the practice if your child does not need this much. It is a nice supplement and review series for any child having reading problems, although some older children I have worked with find the illustrations "babyish."

Beyond the Code

These companions to *Explode the Code* feature decodable stories that follow the phonetic sequence of the series.

Primary Phonics

Levels: Pre-K-2nd grades

Appropriate for: Children with Learning Disabilities or Language Disorders or Slow Learners who are capable of learning phonics.

All students benefit from this program; its individualized nature permits them to progress at their own speed. A set of ten storybooks, each approximately sixteen pages long, accompanies each of the first five workbooks or can be used independently. The storybooks use words containing the phonetic elements taught in the workbooks. As soon as students have learned the short vowel "a," taught in Workbook 1 of **Primary Phonics**, they can read the first storybook, **Mac and Tab**. The newly revised workbooks are progressive in difficulty with constant review to reinforce previously learned material. Used in combination with the storybooks, Primary Phonics introduces reading comprehension at the earliest level of phonetic understanding.

Reading Milestones ***

Levels: K-4th

Appropriate for: Children with Learning Disabilities who are struggling with phonetic approaches (children with severe auditory processing or discrimination difficulties for example), Hearing Impairments, Developmental Disabilities, and Autism.

This is a sight reading program designed for deaf, developmentally disabled, or any other children with severe auditory disabilities. As with any sight program, long-term memory needs to be a relative strength for the child; however, the workbooks do provide some practice in word analysis skills as well as practice in sequencing and comprehension. This is the program I used with my autistic, mentally retarded daughter. The books have delightful illustrations, but there are several stories that deal with dressing up for Halloween as ghosts and witches and these have bothered some of the parents I have shown this program to. I would say that if those stories bother you, skip them, but if you have a child who needs a sight approach to reading, this is definitely the one I would choose.

Teaching Reading to Children with Down Syndrome ***
By Patricia Logan Oelwein
This book provides an excellent method for teaching sight reading to any severely handicapped child. Combine it with the Reading Milestones readers for a complete sight reading program.

Comprehension

Starting Comprehension ***
Levels: Pre K-2nd grade

Appropriate for: Children learning to read, Learning Disabled, or Slow Learners who need work in comprehension well below grade level.

I am so excited about this series of workbooks because someone has finally realized that not all children learn to read in the same way! This series comes in two "strands," visual and phonetic, which allows you to choose your child's strength to reinforce comprehension while working on difficult areas (such as phonics) separately. I have used this set with my children and have been pleased. Like Explode the Code, it includes writing as part of the reading process, which I believe is essential for all children, but especially for those who have any underlying language difficulties.

Reading Comprehension in Varied Subject Matter ***
Levels: Grades 3-12

Appropriate for: Any child who can read at least at a second grade level, but is struggling with comprehension.

This is also a favorite series of mine because it not only gives students a chance to practice good comprehension skills (such as answering questions, identifying the main idea, identifying details, recalling the sequence of events, and vocabulary practice), but it also draws from a wide variety of materials in social studies, science, literature, mathematics, logic, and the arts. You could use many of these articles as springboards to a unit study or additional reading.

Beginning Reasoning & Reading Series
Level: Grades 3-4

Reasoning & Reading Series
Level: Grades 5-8

These four-unit revised workbooks are based on the belief that reasoning, language, and reading comprehension go hand in hand. Each workbook contains units on word meaning, sentence meaning, paragraph meaning, and reasoning skills.

Compensation

Bring the Classics to Life Series ***
Levels: 1st—5th grade reading levels/Jr. High and older interest level

Appropriate for: Older Learning Disabled students struggling with reading skills and comprehension, Slow Learners, older Mentally Retarded students.

Each classic book in this series has been condensed to ten chapters. Pre-reading exercises, comprehension questions, and vocabulary practice accompany each chapter. Designed to help older students experiencing severe reading problems, the illustrations d⌐ ⌐ babyish and the format looks "older."

Pacemaker Curriculum ***

Levels: High School Content/ 4th grade reading level

Appropriate for: High school students working on a basic diploma or preparing for the GED.

This series contains a full High School program of textbooks including English, Literature, Composition, Basic Math, Consumer Math, Algebra, World History, US History, General Science, Biology, Economics, and American Government.

Other Resources

Phonics Plain and Simple available from NATHHAN www.nathhan. com

Remedia Publications www.rempub.com Many simplified practice workbooks for sight words.

Love and Learning www.loveandlearning.com Program specifically created for children with Down Syndrome. Uses video presentation to facilitate attention. Very successful for the families I have had use it.

High Noon Books www.highnoonbooks.com A great selection of recreational reading for older struggling readers.

CHAPTER 30

Understanding and Strengthening Receptive Language Skills

LANGUAGE DISABILITIES ARE both the most common and the most pervasive of all learning difficulties. Since language is the backbone of almost all academic learning and social interaction, language disorders affect just about every area of a child's life.

Language is also an incredibly complex subject (I have several textbooks devoted to all of the intricacies of language). On the other hand, there are some basic concepts that can be easily understood and applied to our everyday teaching. In this section, I want to give you a sense of the most important aspects of Receptive Language (also called Language Processing) to understand and some tools to incorporate into your teaching.

Receptive language skills allow us to take in and comprehend the language directed at us. The child with adequate language processing abilities takes in information correctly and understands it. He thus builds up a base of knowledge which he organizes in various ways such as categorically, sequentially, etc.

These language based organizations in turn allow him to make sense of new information as it is compared and contrasted with his existing knowledge.

On the other hand, children with weak language processing may not take in information correctly in the first place due to poor auditory analysis skills (discrimination and sequencing of sounds) or they may not fully understand the language they hear due to poor vocabulary or poor language organization skills. Because of this, they have an inadequate knowledge base to work from and often have difficulty making sense of new information. Everything that comes in seems "new" instead of being associated with existing knowledge. This lack of organization leads to many difficulties in understanding the systems involved with reading, spelling, and math. The lack of these language-based organizational skills also causes poor language expression—both spoken and written.

The two major areas that demonstrate language processing difficulties are poor vocabulary and comprehension (listening and reading). However, there are other factors which can contribute to a child's difficulty in these areas which need to be taken into consideration. Let's look at these areas first and then turn to looking at how to determine if a student is having language processing difficulties and what to do about them.

Other Factors to Consider

1. Attention

It can be very difficult to distinguish between a child with poor processing and a child with an attention disorder since reduced attention also creates many comprehension difficulties. It is not unusual for a child who has only an attention problem to do poorly in a classroom setting, but have very few academic difficulties once he comes home to school. For kids like this, the distractions and noise in a classroom reduce their comprehension because they are unable to attend well—not because they are having difficulty with language processing.

At home, children who are struggling academically are usually already in a situation where distractions are reduced. Children with severe attention difficulties may need a very guided, structured routine in order to do well academically— even if there are no indications of a language difficulty. Students who have both attention and language difficulties are among the most difficult children to work with. In this case, the attention difficulties compound the language problems making just about every aspect of school difficult.

Here are some "rules of thumb" to help differentiate the problems you are dealing with:

- If your child was labeled LD in a classroom, but performs fine at home, assume a mild attention disorder
- If your child does well academically, but ONLY with you sitting right by his side keeping him on task, assume a severe attention problem
- If your child struggles academically—especially with comprehension, memory, and written work, but is a hard worker and works well on his own, assume a language disorder
- If your child struggles academically even with you sitting right beside him keeping him on task, assume that both attention and language are issues. You will probably want to address the attention difficulties first so that you can more effectively work on language processing difficulties

2. Lack of Experience/Stimulation

Language is a building up of a knowledge base. Children who have not had a variety of rich, personal experiences tend to have an impoverished vocabulary and comprehension. Among home schooled children this is probably not the primary cause for vocabulary and comprehension difficulties as it might be for children in some other settings. However, I mention it because if a child is demonstrating vocabulary and comprehension difficulties, it is important to look critically and make sure that we are providing a wide variety of experiences which provide meaning to the language in the child's environment. I know from my own personal experience how much extra work it is to take my autistic daughter places and involve her in the experiences that are commonplace for other children, and I often wonder if she really "gets anything out of it." But I keep reminding myself that it is worth the effort because every experience she has adds to the amount of language she may be able to comprehend and use.

A related issue is that of adequate stimulation. Some children do not receive enough language directed at them, and this can make them appear to have a language disorder when they are really just being under stimulated. Again, this is more than likely not a problem among home schooled families because of the high degree of parent concern and involvement. However, it is still a good reminder to all of us as to the importance of simply talking to our children. It is a fact that children who speak well are spoken to more than children who speak poorly or not at all. Unfortunately, it is the children who speak poorly or who speak very little who are the ones who need to be spoken to the most. I do know, however, that it is very easy to neglect to talk to quiet children. This is however one case where the saying "If it's not broke, don't fix it" definitely does not apply!

Assessing Language Processing Difficulties

As mentioned earlier, there are three main areas of language processing: auditory analysis skills, vocabulary, and comprehension. Of course these can all be tested formally by a professional, but for those parents who would like to explore their child's language skills themselves. Jerome Rosner's book *Helping Children Overcome Learning Difficulties* is an excellent resource. Unfortunately, this excellent book is no longer easy to get a hold of. Check on amazon.com for used copies or check your local library.

In this book, Rosner gives a very simple test for determining auditory skills called the "Test of Auditory Analysis Skills." This test looks at the child's ability to identify separate sounds in words and the sequence of sounds in a word. It is appropriate for children at kindergarten age and above.

Additionally, Rosner gives a very simple language test for assessing receptive vocabulary, expressive vocabulary, and basic comprehension. It is appropriate for children age three and older. The skills demonstrated stop at an 8-year-old age level because Rosner believes assessing language above that level gets very complex, but if you have an older child struggling with language, you would still be able to tell if he was having difficulty at the basic levels.

Another book that gives some similar (though not as detailed) information on assessing auditory skills is Sheldon Rappaport's book, *How to Teach Your Child to Read and Spell Successfully,* which is available on my website (www.avcsbooks.com).

What to Do

1. Work on Auditory Skills. Some good resources include:

- Auditory Skills Training in Rosner book pp. 189 – 210
- Listen My Children—auditory accuracy (AVCS Books catalog – request at www.avcsbooks.com)
- Help 1—auditory discrimination exercises (LinguiSystems 1.800.776.4332 www.linguisystems. com)
- HELP 4—Talking About Language (LinguiSystems)
- HELP for Auditory Processing—sounds in words (LinguiSystems)

2. Work on Vocabulary.

Children should be able to define any word in a reader at the level they are reading. For pre-readers, vocabulary work is usually termed "concepts." Here are some resources for strengthening vocabulary skills.

Concept Skills: Preschool to grade 2
- Many items in the LinguiSystems catalog (1.800.776.4332 www.linguisystems.com) such as: Scissors, Glue and Concepts, Too; The Best Concept Workbook Ever
- Opposites section in *Phonics Plain and Simple* (NATHHAN 208.267.6246) www.nathhan.com

Vocabulary Skills
- No Glamour Vocabulary (and many more titles) LinguiSystems (ages 8 and up)
- Activities in Rosner book pp. 106 – 113 K and up

- Wordly Wise (EPS www.epsbooks.com) All grades
- Reading Comprehension in Varied Subject Matter (AVCS Books) grades 2 – 12
- Use any spelling program to work on vocabulary by requiring words to be defined and used—not just spelled by rote.

3. Work on Language-based Organizational Skills.

The reason for working on these types of skills is to "teach children how to use words to organize thoughts so they are easier to remember" (Rosner p. 113). These skills include:

a. categorizing
b. sequencing
c. ordering (such as alphabetizing)
d. memory strategies
e. visualization skills

Resources include:
- Starting Comprehension—Sequencing skills K – 2nd (www.avcsbooks.com)
- The HELP series (LinguiSystems) ages 6 – adult
- AlphaBetter—(most home school catalogs) 3rd grade skills and above
- Reading Comprehension in Varied Subject Matter (sequencing) grades 2-12 (www.avcsbooks.com)
- Visualizing and Verbalizing - all ages (www.avcsbooks. com)

CHAPTER 31

Understanding and Strengthening Expressive Language Skills

EXPRESSIVE LANGUAGE INVOLVES speaking (oral language) and writing (written language). Written language is one of the most complex academic tasks because it coordinates visual-motor skills, language skills, and cognitive skills. Thus, it is usually the last form of communication to be mastered.

There are three basic components of expressive language:

Usage: This refers to grammar both spoken and written. There is informal usage such as is used in everyday speech and formal grammar used in writing. For most people, only the formal grammar of writing has to be directly taught, but many special needs children also need direct instruction in the basic rules of spoken grammar (such as plurals, pronouns, endings).

Mechanics: The rules of written language—spelling, capitalization, and punctuation. Most of these rules have evolved in order to make reading easier (consistent spelling, sentence and paragraph divisions) and more understandable (most comma rules), but don't forget that there are some rules that have no

237

relation to either organization of understanding but are merely conventions (the rules surrounding quotations). For example, the following sentence does not change meaning if we put the period inside or outside the quotation marks: Mary said, "I saw the boy." However, the comma in the following sentence is essential to the meaning of the sentence: In reading, comprehension will be impaired by poor vocabulary. If we take the comma out, the sentence has no meaning.

Organization: Organization refers to formulating expressive products (both spoken and written) that are "logical, coherent, and sequenced." This could be an oral story or summary, a letter, a creative story, or a more formal report. Immature expressive language tends to be disjointed in sequence and incomplete in detail. Mature expression, on the other hand, is carefully and clearly developed and contains stylistic elements such as transitions and examples to aid the listener's or reader's understanding. At a mature level, a person's organization also takes on a personal style marked by creativity and the development of themes in a way that is distinctive to that person. You can't really teach this.

The basic theme of teaching children with learning problems should be "Don't Despair," but this seems to be especially true of teaching expressive language skills. It is entirely common for children to learn the correct subject pronouns, but revert to saying "Her went with us," when trying to relate a story to Grandma. It is even more usual for a child to complete a worksheet on capitals correctly, spell specific words accurately on Tuesday, and produce a written paragraph on Friday that looks as if capitalization, punctuation, and spelling have never been taught in his lifetime! These frustrating truths are due in part to the standard "memory leaks" that all learning disabled children struggle with, and in part to the highly complex, integrative nature of written language. Thus, as in all aspects of teaching our children, we must employ a good basic skills framework, teach the skills, and review these skills constantly.

Let's now turn to looking at the specifics of teaching oral and written communication.

Oral Language

I believe in starting with oral language skills first before trying to do too much with written language. For an older child, it may not be entirely practical to work on only oral language first, but at least a time of putting away writing and working only orally can be very helpful to the struggling older child. Before trying to teach writing skills, make sure your child can do the following:

- Repeat Sentences
- Describe a picture using a complete, grammatically correct sentence in all verb tenses (past, present, future) and with regular and irregular constructions.
- Repeat a three to four sentence paragraph
- Give an oral summary of a story and be able to tell the main idea.

Some resources to help you plan in this area:
- Scissors, Glue and Grammar, Too (or any of the oral grammar resources from LinguiSystems – www.linguisystems.com)
- Listen My Children – AVCS Books Catalog - request a catalog at www.avcsbooks.com
- Visualizing and Verbalizing www.avcsbooks.com

Basic Written Language

Once a child is at a solid second grade reading/speaking level, he is ready to start some written language instruction. As you move into written language keep in mind that you are going to be doing many different things all at once. Take it slow and easy and don't panic.

In teaching written language, I like to start with copying instead of creating writing. The reason is that writing is very complex. So we need a way to teach the basics of mechanics, usage, and organization without the additional angst that comes with asking them to come up with creative ideas out of their own heads! But seriously, combining creativity with writing skills is truly difficult, and even more so for kids with learning problems. This is the reason that I really like to start out with a program like *Learning Language Arts Through Literature* (Common Sense Press) so that all of the basic skills can be taught and practiced from good writing by other authors. This is a time-honored method for teaching writing skills. Both Ben Franklin and George Washington taught themselves the basics of writing and style by copying other writers' works and eventually by re-writing other writers' works in their own words. *A Strong Start in Language* by Ruth Beechick also discusses the benefits of this approach and is a great resource to have on hand.

Of course, for most students with learning problems, this will not be enough practice and repetition. Here are some other good resources for teaching the basics. (More detailed reviews of some of the programs will be given at the end of this section.)

- How To Teach Spelling and the How to Spell workbooks www.avcsbooks.com

- Winston Grammar (www.winstongrammar.com) a multi-sensory, color coding system for comprehending grammar concepts
- Easy Grammar and Daily Grams www.avcsbooks.com
- No Glamour Grammar www.linguisystems.com
- The Apple Tree Language Program www.avcsbooks. com

This is also the time to start what I call pre-creative writing by having your student dictate stories to you and then recopy them, and by writing friendly letters to (uncritical) relatives.

Creative Written Language

By the time a student is working at approximately a fourth grade level he should begin putting sentences together into paragraphs and then move into longer, more creative writing. The biggest problems that most learning disabled students run into at this level are putting their thoughts into a logical sequence and thinking of something to write! I'll start with the most basic programs that teach the organization of writing and work up to the idea books that just give writing projects. Of course, there will be some overlap.

- Teaching Competence in Written Language (especially for severely disabled students needing basic writing skills) www.avcsbooks.com
- The Paragraph Books www.avcsbooks.com
- Critical Thinking Press 1.800.458.4849 www.criticalthinking.com has great resources for ideas and challenging writing such as *Critical Thinking to Improve Writing Skills* (above 4th grade level)

RESOURCES

Resources available from AVCS Books (www.avcsbooks.com or our print catalog). If an item is starred (***) it is available on the website. If not, it is available in the catalog. You can request a catalog on the website.

How to Teach Spelling *** How to Spell (accompanying workbooks)

Levels: Grades 1-12

Appropriate for: Learning and Language Disabilities.

This is my favorite spelling program. First of all, it is a complete 1st to 12th grade program. Secondly, it is designed to systematically teach the rules and generalizations of spelling, not just memorizing lists of words. Testing is done through dictated sentences which check rules previously taught as well as those in the current lesson. This is a very meaty program, and the teacher's manual can look overwhelming at first glance. Following the sequence in the workbooks and going to the teacher's manual for dictation materials only makes this program easier to use initially. The instructions at the beginning of the book are intended for a classroom and should be modified to fit your home situation and specific needs of your child.

Teaching spelling, no matter what you use, to kids with language learning disabilities can be very discouraging! Realistically, many children with language difficulties will never be "good" spellers. If you go through a good program and emphasize memorizing (as best they can) the rules of spelling, they will be able to get close enough so that items such as spell-checkers or Franklin spellers will be useful tools. I recommend that you make charts, posters, or lists (maybe with art work by your child) of the spelling rules as they are studied. Then encourage your child to refer to their own rule list as they encounter difficult words. In this way, the information is constantly in front of them to review and use, which is more functional than just having a lot of memorized rules without knowing how to use them.

Spelling Power

Levels: 2nd grade reading level and up

Appropriate for: Learning Disabled students

This multi-sensory spelling program is based on mastering the 5,000 most frequently used words. Children work at their own pace for fifteen minutes a day. Although not written for LD kids—and many of our kids will never "master" all of these words—the format is easily adaptable for children with learning challenges.

Megawords

Levels: 4th grade skills and above

Appropriate for: Learning disabled students who need remediation in spelling and reading multisyllabic words.

Easy Grammar and Daily Grams

Levels: Grades 2-12

Appropriate for: Mildly Learning Disabled, may need some modifications

This is a complete program for teaching and reviewing basic grammar skills. The Easy Grammar text systematically teaches the elements of grammar (the text and workbooks are identical except that the workbook does not contain the answer key), and the Daily Grams provides an introduction to grammar at the lower levels (2nd-3rd) and review at the higher levels so that mastery can be maintained.

Easy Writing

Lower Elementary to basic High School skills

This book teaches students how to write a variety of complex sentence structures. The text is divided into two distinct levels: lower and upper elementary sentence skills, and upper elementary through basic high school sentence skills. It provides excellent instruction and ample sentence writing practice.

The Paragraph Books ***

Level: 3rd grade and up

Appropriate for: Students needing to learn basic paragraph skills

This series' step-by-step approach builds writing competency from the ground up—students learn to edit, format, and build paragraphs while mastering 4 basic writing strands. By the end of the book, students are writing complete essays. Lively writing, illustrations, and a systematic approach make this series easy to teach and to use. *The Paragraph Book* series is especially useful for students with weak writing/motor skills who have trouble with handwriting. Through ample practice with editing marks, students learn the material without becoming worn out or frustrated with the process of writing and rewriting. This method has been tested and shown to work with LD students of varying levels, as well as other students. This series is also beneficial for students with organizational problems; the structured format gives them a framework on which to build. Students who have difficulty spotting errors will also find this program helpful. Special attention is given to looking for missing capitals, dropped endings, missing and double words, etc. This is a great aid to those with weak symbol systems.

The Four Square Writing Method

Levels: 1st—9th grade level writing skills

Appropriate for: Learning Disabled students needing a concrete approach to learning writing skills.

This series provides yet another format for visual, concrete instruction in writing. Using a "square" as a visual cue—students are taught to fill in the boxes before writing to organize their thoughts.

Apple Tree Language Program ***

Levels: 1st— 3rd grade reading levels

Appropriate for: Students reading at approx. 1st— 3rd grade levels who are struggling with basic writing skills.

A structured, sequential approach to developing good sentence structure as the basis for written language skills. I like the many pictures and charts used throughout this program which help clarify structures that children with language problems find confusing. The teacher's manual explains the abbreviations used in the workbooks (although they are not too hard - V is for verb!) and gives teaching ideas aimed more at a classroom format. Most home schoolers find they do not need the teacher's manual.

Teaching Competence in Written Language

Levels: 4th-9th grade writing skills

Appropriate for: Mildly Learning Disabled students needing to learn competent writing.

This manual provides a very complete and systematic writing program from the sentence level through essays. I especially like the many charts and structured format pages to help students gain an understanding of the organizational structures being taught. Although the initial price looks daunting, this program is meaty and would take most LD students several years to master. Additional materials would be needed to teach research writing to high school students, but this is a very complete program up to that point.

Writing Skills ***

Students practice writing sentences and developing paragraphs through writing about their ideas and personal experiences. A logical sequence of writing skills takes students from individual sentences to basic paragraphs of five sentences, expanded paragraphs, and essays.

Visualizing and Verbalizing for Language Comprehension and Thinking *** *By Nanci Bell*
The Visualizing and Verbalizing manual provides theory and specific steps to develop concept imagery— the ability to image a gestalt (whole). The program applies concept imagery to reading comprehension, oral language comprehension, following directions, high order thinking skills, expressive language, and writing.

Other Resources:

Editor in Chief – Critical Thinking Press (www.critialthinking.com)

Proofreading practice for students who needs to practice proofreading skills, but don't need as much copying practice as is in Learning Language Arts Through Literature

CHAPTER 32

Understanding and Strengthening Math Skills

CHILDREN WHO HAVE difficulty with math present different challenges than those encountered in the reading and language areas. Often with reading or writing difficulties, we can continue building on content even if the independent reading or writing level remains low. In math, however, there is no way that we can continue on in content until lower level skills have been mastered or at least understood to the point that they can be utilized (even if not memorized!). Thus, it is common for parents to feel that their child is "way behind" because there is such a clear, sequential progression to mathematics.

Let's first look at the typical progression for learning math skills, and then at the ways that learning problems affect math performance. Finally, we will look at methods for working with math dysfunction and the curricula best suited for different types of learning difficulties.

NOTE: The bulk of the next two sections has been summarized from two books: *Developing Number Concepts*

Using Unifix Cubes, and *Teaching Mathematics to Students with Learning Disabilities.* Both are fabulous resources and highly recommended.

Development of Math Skills

Number Concept: The beginnings of number concept include a number of different notions, but the general concept is that "number is an idea" which can't be seen. It is this abstract nature of math that makes it so difficult for some children. The mastery of these basic concepts makes it possible to move on to being able to use numbers in meaningful ways. While most children are comfortable with these basic concepts by the mental age of about nine, more severely handicapped children may never completely master these basic concepts, and other learning disabled children may grasp the concepts only superficially which impedes higher level mathematical reasoning skills. Number concept as a whole is made up of the following concepts:

1. Classification—the ability to sort by specific properties into consistent categories
2. Ordering—the ability to organize materials in a logical sequence. Rote counting is not ordering. To truly understand ordering, a child must understand the concepts of more, less, before, after. Then they have to be able to put numbers, items, or problem steps in order even if they are presented out of order.
3. Inclusion—the idea that "three" includes items one and two, it is not the name of the object
4. One-to-One Correspondence—the idea that you must say or think only one word for each object

5. Conservation—The idea that the number of objects does not change if the objects are moved, rearranged, or hidden

6. Connecting Symbols to the Number Concept—recognizing that the symbol "4" means 4 objects, and then being able to write the numbers to represent a group of objects. (This is different than just learning to write numbers—that is a handwriting task.)

Basic Operations: After children master the basics of number concept, they move on to learning how to manipulate numbers through the four basic operations of addition, subtraction, multiplication, and division. In order to understand these number manipulations, the ideas of ordering (e.g. when adding the numbers get larger) and one-to-one correspondence must be expanded upon, and new concepts such as place value need to be understood. At this stage, we are talking about simply computing numbers to gain an answer. There are students with learning difficulties who understand the process of basic operations, but are unsuccessful in computation because of spatial difficulties in lining up problems or motor difficulties in writing answers. For these students, calculators are invaluable and highly recommended to allow moving on to the more crucial aspects of problem solving and applications.

Problem Solving (Application): The next step, and one that most children with learning problems have difficulty with, is moving from simply computing numbers to solving problems. This is the point at which a student can interpret given information and decide how to solve the problem. In order to do this, the student must understand what the problem is, what information is relevant and irrelevant to solving the problem, which operation is needed, and whether the solution he arrives at is reasonable. This process involves integrating many skills such as language, sequencing, patterning, and reasoning. Often we think of this area as just "word problems," but most "real-life" mathematics involves these skills. Using time and money concepts on a day to day basis requires application skills. For example, consider the integration of skills needed to even accurately assess something simple like what time it will be one hour from now. First, it takes language skills to understand that "an hour from now" is an addition problem, sequencing skills to determine the next number, and the possibility of both patterning (how is a clock constructed) and reasoning skills if it is now 12:00 to know that the next hour will be 1:00 not 13:00!

Methods

Working with students having difficulty in math involves three basic things: Simplify, Repeat, and Vary. Since math builds on itself, repetition is a necessary, but often frustrating part of having a child with a math "problem!" Always remember to relax and move at your child's pace. Let go of worrying about being "ahead" or "behind" and concentrate on giving your child the best math understanding he is capable of.

Simplify: Employ techniques that minimize the effect of the learning problem.
- Use manipulatives and charts to make abstract concepts more concrete
- Use visual cues to assist students with figure-ground and other perceptual difficulties: Graph paper, lines, boxes, color coding, large problems

- Balance computation and application problems. Allow calculators when doing application problems. This minimizes both frustration and errors.
- Concentrate on the most practical aspects of math. Working a problem correctly is practical—Speed Drills are not practical

Repeat: Review concepts and procedures many times.
- Solidify basic number concepts (with very young or disabled children, this may be all you can do)
- Introduce new material in small chunks
- Don't be afraid to move slowly—at the pace your child needs

Vary: Use a good variety of materials to review concepts.
- Games
- Computers
- Drill activities
- Real-life situations

Thinking and reasoning skills are related to math problem solving skills. Even though this is not "math," working in this area can be helpful. Always begin by working on thinking and reasoning skills using your child's strong area (verbal or nonverbal), and then move into his weak area. Critical Thinking Press has many great resources for building reasoning skills. One good general resource is the "Building Thinking Skills" series, but they also carry reasoning skill books directly related to math. Logic problems and thought puzzles (such as tangrams) or spatial puzzles (for children with spatial as well as reasoning difficulties) are also excellent for building problem solving skills and flexible thinking.

RESOURCES

Resources available from AVCS Books www.avcsbooks.com or our print catalog. If an item is starred (***) it is available on the website. If not, it is available in the catalog. You can request a catalog on the website.

Developing Number Concepts *** *By Kathy Richardson*
Levels: Math concepts for grade levels K-3

Appropriate for: Any child needing either initial or remedial in basic math concepts as long as manipulatives are not distracting to the child.

This is a comprehensive core math program that utilizes manipulatives in flexible ways to build number concepts and operation skills. This revised edition includes the use of a variety of manipulatives in addition to the Unifix Cubes. Each activity is explained in an easy to understand format and is well illustrated— a gold mine of ideas for teaching and reviewing number concepts.

Teaching Mathematics to Students with Learning Disabilities

This book is aimed at helping teachers in regular and special education setting adapt the mathematics curriculum to meet the needs of students with learning disabilities. Topics include time, money concepts, computation involving whole numbers, rational numbers, percentages, and computer programs that are suited for mathematics students with learning disabilities.

On Cloud Nine: Visualizing and Verbalizing for Math *by Tuley and Bell*

On Cloud Nine explains how to use the Lindamood-Bell visual imagery techniques to develop underlying math concepts for reasoning and problem solving with numbers. Beginning with the most basic concepts of counting, addition, subtraction, multiplication, and division; the steps progress to word problems, fractions, and decimals.

Recipe for Math ***

Levels: 1st-6th grades, remedial

Appropriate for: Learning Disabled and Language Disabilities

Recipe for Math consists of a comprehensive teacher's manual that gives daily lesson plans, goals, and objectives for each concept (so you know exactly why you are doing each activity) and one of the best explanations of why math is difficult for children with language difficulties that I've ever seen, as well as practice workbooks. Game suggestions and directions are given, and the author has great ideas for making math accessible to children with language disabilities (such as color coding the direction to work the problems).

Modern Curriculum Press

We are often asked for a complete math curriculum, and Modern Curriculum Press is a good basic presentation with a fairly good amount of work space.

If your student needs more practice in a particular area, supplement with Attack Math, Touch Math, or Key to Math workbooks.

Attack Math ***

Levels: 1st-5th computation skills

Appropriate for: Learning Disabled, Language Disabilities, any child needing to solidify basic computation skills.

This workbook series gets my highest recommendation for its clear step-by-step presentation of basic computations skills and its large problems on uncluttered pages. Excellent for children with motor difficulties or visual perception difficulties as well as those who need a very systematic presentation of basic skills. Every arithmetic operation is covered in 3 books. Book 1 teaches basic facts and books 2 and 3 teach multi-digit computation with whole numbers.

Touch Math ***

Levels: K-3rd

Appropriate for: Severely Disabled, Highly Visual Learners who have difficulty with number concepts

This counting method of teaching basic addition and subtraction uses "Touch Points" on each number to assist students in remembering and associating number value. Addition and subtraction is taught as a process of counting forwards and backwards by using the touch points on each number

Keys to Math ***

Students work at their own pace in these uncluttered paperback workbooks. Concepts build gradually and include fractions, decimals, algebra, and geometry. Great for older kids who need a more basic approach to the more difficult math concepts.

"Fun Way" Math by *Judy Liautaud and Dave Rodriguez*

These books use a picture-story method that is designed to aid retention. A picture and story with each lesson allow students to recall the addition and multiplication math facts more easily

Calculadder

Levels: 1st-6th grade math calculation skills

Appropriate for: Students needing repetition and practice in basic math skills

These worksheets provide an easy way to review and practice calculation skills from addition through division. Some of the pages have better spacing than others, and some pages are unfortunately crowded with problems. You can pick and choose appropriate pages for students with visual or motor difficulties. Pages could also be enlarged. I would also ignore the time limit set at the bottom of the page for most LD students.

It's Elementary!

Levels: 2nd— 5th grade skills

Appropriate for: Students with language disorders, having a hard time with word problems.

This series teaches students a reliable method for analyzing and solving word problems. Students learn to identify keywords, draw pictures, and disregard unnecessary information. The book covers each of the four operations: book 1 single digits, book 2 double digits, and book 3 advanced arithmetic.

Understanding Math Story Problems ***

Levels: 2nd-4th grade reading levels

Appropriate for: Students with language based learning disabilities

Teaches students the vocabulary needed to understand and solve math story problems. All four basic operations (addition, subtraction, multiplication, and division) are covered.

Mind Benders

PreK-K through Grade 12

These workbooks contain deductive thinking puzzles for help in developing mental organizational skills and logic. The key is to start with the most obvious associations, then deduce less obvious associations until everything finally fits together.

Other Math Resources:

Mastering Mathematics www.masterypublications.com

From their website:

"Students learn one basic skill at a time - at their own pace - up to their potential - until it is mastered. Then they review this skill in the next book. Skills aren't divided into artificial, foolish tidbits (called "grade levels"). With no jumping from skill to skill, confusion is eliminated.

Mastering Mathematics has a balanced approach.

Manipulatives of durable cardstock are easily assembled. As children progress and "outgrow" them, you don't end up with a lot of expensive, "pretty plastic." Plus, younger children won't choke on them.

Workbooks then help your child put his learning on paper (the place where he will demonstrate his mastery throughout life). All work pages face a blank left page so children can focus on problems they need to solve today, not yesterday's work. These consumable (and reproducible) texts have large print, allowing more room to write big answers with little hands. Most pages have no more than twenty problems—enough to master the skill, but not so many to discourage the child.

Games reinforce fact memorization, making math "friendlier." Games are also used to teach equivalent facts for time, money, measurement, metric, and geometry terminology instead of boring work sheets."

CHAPTER 33

What Is the Best Curriculum to Use?

For all of you now reeling from the many resources available, here is some "food for thought" from the "Frequently Asked Questions" page of our website.

THE BEST CURRICULUM is the one you modify to fit the unique needs of your child. There are no perfect curricula, so I think a better question is "What are the most important teaching techniques to use with my special needs child?" I emphasize this because while no curriculum can solve learning difficulties, solid teaching will take your child to his or her potential.

In general, you will be creating a group of resources based on your child's weaknesses, interests, and strengths. Meet your child where he/she is. If he is in 5th grade, but can only read himself at 1st grade level, then use remedial reading and low level/high interest reading material (such as "Bring the Classics to Life") to work on reading, but read history, science, and literature to him (or get textbooks on tape from Recording for the Blind and Dyslexic www.rfbd.org) at his comprehension level.

The most important thing you can do when teaching a child with learning problems is to make them think up to their intellectual potential. Almost all children with learning struggles are passive learners. They truly believe that unless information just soaks into their heads, there is nothing they can do to aid the learning process!

Our job as teachers is to activate our children to become as engaged as possible in the learning process. No matter what curriculum you use, you engage your child by asking questions and pushing them past their "I don't knows." The two most important questions to ask any child are: "What does this mean?" and "How are you going to remember this?" Now, with more severely disabled students, these questions may not be feasible, but even my autistic daughter can be pushed to engage in the learning process by my asking her questions and not allowing her to do things the same way every time we do a task. This forces thinking—even on her limited level—to take place.